THE

CONDO BIBLE

FOR AMERICANS

You will confer the greatest benefits on your city,
not by raising its roofs, but by exalting its souls.

For it is better that great souls
should live in small habitations than that abject
slaves should burrow in great houses.

—EPICTETUS, C. 110

THE CONDO BIBLE

FOR AMERICANS

EVERYTHING YOU MUST KNOW
BEFORE AND AFTER BUYING A CONDO

DAN S. BARNABIC

NEON-PUBLISHING CORP.

Cataloguing in Publication data available from Library of Congress.

ISBN 978-0-9868651-1-4

Editorial Assistant: Sandro Xavier Otegui
Cover design: Christian Otegui/Gnibel
Text design and typesetting: Daniel Crack, Kinetics Design, kdbooks.ca

Photo credits:

Page 13, www.shutterstock.com: albund.

Pages 15–45, www.istockphoto.com: 15, JazzIRT; 17, TimAbramowitz;
19, Chepkol; 23, sqback; p. 25, Bet_Noire; 28, SimmiSimons; 30,
Cimmerian; 33, FreeTransform; 36, VikaValter; 41, joecicak; 44,
luismmolina.

Neon-Publishing Corp.
Toronto, Canada
Tel: 647-347-1773
Fax: 416-921-9617
www.condobible.com
info@condobible.com

CONTENTS

2 THE REALITIES OF CONDO LIFE 47

6 RECOMMENDED REFORMS TO THE CONDO SYSTEM 163

CONCLUSION 179

APPENDIX: THE HISTORY OF CO-OPS: A CAUTIONARY TALE 181

REFERENCES 189

INTRODUCTION

I have written *The Condo Bible for Americans* as a *buyer beware* and an *owner beware* book on condominiums. In keeping with this mission, the book was written based on an almost forgotten fact that the very concept of condominum-like ownership previously failed on a massive scale between the First and Second World Wars. The ownership concept was known as a co-ownership, cooperative, or "co-op" – an arrangement very similar to the present-day condominium. In fact, the story behind the massive failure of co-ops inspired this book; the public needs a cautionary tale about present-day condominium ownership.

The condominium ownership structure is, for most people, convoluted, ambiguous, and to a large extent, misleading as developers, builders, legal advisors, and government agencies typically fail to adequately address the unavoidable shortcomings that often result from condo-minium ownership. Its pitfalls and shortcomings – which will be explained in the pages ahead – and the ability to deal with them will play a pivotal role in the preservation of condominium values in years to come.

This book:

- Starts you off with the Ten Commandments of Condo Buying, a preview of many must-check items and valuable tips on what to watch for when buying a condo unit

- Explains in detail the practical realities of condo ownership and its inherent problems

- Compares owning a condo with owning a house

- Examines owning a condo vs. renting an apartment, putting to the test the commonly held belief that a renter should always strive to buy a property, particularly with regard to buying a condominium

- Answers the proverbial question, "How long will condos last?"

- Analyzes ownership as an investment; as a speculative real estate product; and as a personal residence with reference to condo affordability factors. It also provides numerous other valuable pieces of information and statistics

- Provides valuable practical remedial measures and recommendations for both unit owners and condo boards facing ongoing challenges associated with condo ownership

The Condo Bible for Americans is intended to serve as an eye-opener both for consumers seeking to own or who already own a condo and those working in government and financial institutions who are involved in regulation and governance issues related to condo ownership.

In addition, the appendix of the book deals in more detail with the origins of condominiums in cooperatives – apartments bought by renters – a real estate phenomenon that emerged and failed between the two world wars of the 20th century and that exists to the present day, albeit overshadowed by the overwhelming popularity and proliferation ... of condominiums.

I first started to sense the problems inherent in condominium ownership as a real estate agent in 1973. After progressing to co-own a real estate brokerage firm by 1976, I became involved in the field of property management. In 1985 I joined a real estate investors' group and became a condo developer and head of acquisition and management. In 1990 I exited the real estate industry after becoming one of the many victims of the massive real estate depression of the time. Since that time, I became a keen observer of condo proliferation and consumer advocate on matters of credit reporting and personal finance issues. My concern over many failed condominium ownerships at the time grew to the point of my deciding to pen my own thoughts on the subject. For the following 20 years, I compiled – in stages and from knowledge acquired in the field and later on through research – the information needed for writing this book.

Now let me set the context for you regarding the popularity of condos today.

The Condo Explosion

For the first five decades of the 20th century, and for centuries before that, two basic options were available to those seeking living arrangements: rent an apartment or purchase a house.

But along with the Beatles, bell-bottom pants, and the muscle car, a new kind of habitat product exploded on the North American scene in the mid-1960s: the condominium.

At first blush, buying a condo unit seems to offer the best of both worlds. Condo residents own their unit, yet, unlike traditional homeowners, they don't have to worry about maintenance issues such as landscaping or infrastructure repairs. It's a "no muss, no fuss" way to live.

However, since there is no such thing as a free ride, condominium owners are obligated to pay monthly maintenance fees, which are channeled toward the overall upkeep of the common elements of the condominium complex. This monthly payment has parallels to renting an apartment.

Nevertheless, condominium life has proven to be popular from the outset. Condos quickly grew from a mere trickle to today's deluge of developments. An increasing number of people, especially those living in congested urban and tourist areas of major cities and resorts, have been eagerly buying in to the sales pitches of condominium developers.

Buyers bought with apparent good reason. The condominium lifestyle does offer some obvious advantages. Typically, condo units are ideal residences for those without children. They are also well suited to older individuals weary of the constant chores that come with traditional home ownership. Indeed, the explosion of condominiums of different kinds and shapes is proving to have been well timed for the aging postwar generation – that large cohort of people we all know as the baby boomers, who are increasingly looking for hassle-free living.

More and more boomers will be reaching retirement age over the next several years, and a significant number of them will embrace the condominium lifestyle. This explains why condo developments continue to surge in most cities across North America; they may even outnumber overall traditional housing startups in the near future.

The Perils of Condominiums

Yet, despite the many obvious advantages that go hand-in-hand with owning a condominium, such an investment can also be fraught with peril. In fact, many of the inherent disadvantages of condominium ownership are not known by the general public. Often, these disadvantages and shortfalls become serious enough to adversely affect a condo unit's value.

For starters, the passage of time inevitably leads to physical wear and tear on condo complexes, leading to more frequent and more extensive (and expensive) repairs. Ironically, those who shun home ownership because they see a house as a money pit may not be that much better off owning a condo.

Other and far more serious adverse factors stem from the very nature of the condominium's communal ownership structure: its dependence on the economic diversity of the complex's cohabitants, the quality of its common-element governance, and prevailing economic conditions, all of which are beyond an individual unit owner's control.

Ultimately, economic diversity among condo unit owners and the ability to buy condominium units for little or no down payment will play a major role in determining the overall fiscal health of condominium complexes in the future.

Condominium unit owners know that buyers who put little or no equity into their units are typically the first to lose their units should the economy tank. What they may not know is that a complex's accumulation of debt due to non-payment of maintenance and assessment fees could also spell financial hardship for *non-defaulting* owners, including the devaluation of their unit. To put it simply, one defaulting unit owner automatically affects all non-defaulting unit owners.

The average consumer isn't likely to research potential problems associated with owning a condominium, which is quite different from owning a traditional freehold property. This book draws attention to the differences to help you be more knowledgeable, whether you are interested in buying in to a communal ownership arrangement or have already done so. This is the very *raison d'être* of this book. It is intended to be an informative guide to understanding residential condominiums.

As you will see throughout the book, you are advised to take condo-marketing schemes with a grain of salt. In their zeal to sell as many units as possible, developers and the financial sector are facilitating condo purchases with very low or even no down payments. They are luring renters to reallocate their monthly rental payments toward building their own equity as opposed to enriching their landlord. Their sales pitches have prompted into condo ownership scores of tenants who are financially ill prepared to become their own landlords.

The obvious problem with these purchase arrangements is that the jobs traditional renters hold may not be secure in the long term. Their earnings may plummet, leaving them with little or no cash reserves, rendering them vulnerable to even the slightest economic downturn. These people are especially prone to defaulting on their monthly financial obligations, such as taxes, maintenance fees, and mortgage payments.

It gets worse. As the segment of condominium owners who purchased their units with small or no down payments increases – and there are indications that, as of 2007, close to 40 percent of such small- or no-equity owners had already bought into condominium complexes – many complexes may eventually become part of the professional speculators' inventory and thus be liable to takeovers during times of low demand and adverse market conditions.

In fact, it is possible that a widespread condominium failure may follow in the wake of serious economic shake-downs such as interest rate spikes, increased unemployment, or oversupply (a major culprit in any real estate market drop). The fallout from no-equity owners will undoubtedly result in considerable losses for owners who are left behind.

To put this into perspective, take a look at this trend in the United States.

By mid-2006, certain urban areas had reached a state of satiety. By September 2007, according to the S&P/ Case-Shiller Home Price Index, housing sales fell in 40 states, posting the steepest price drop in 16 years, making it obvious that the market had gone into a state of "correction."[1] In fact, by 2011, the market was still very depressed, with signs of recovery starting to show in 2013. Market correction, a gentle term for price deflation, occurs when affordability is being pushed to the absolute margin and the market becomes overextended. Historically, markets frequently go through stages of correction of varying lengths of time. The last major corrections of the market occurred in the early 1990s and 2006 when real estate values plummeted as much as 30 percent in many urban areas.

Developers' insatiable thirst to convert as many existing rental apartment buildings into condominiums as possible compounded yet another long-existing problem – the depletion of affordable rental housing. Given the proven inability of governments to meet demands for affordable rental housing, this problem alone could lead to future social and economic upheavals, fueled by the "working poor."

The conditions for such a scenario already exist. Just look at the record number of heavily indebted and impoverished Americans. According to the U.S. government, more than an estimated 35 million of them struggled financially in 2005. The Census Bureau's American Community Survey pegged the Miami poverty rate in 2006 to be at 26.9 percent, way above the state of Florida's average of 9 percent.[2] A

1 Standard & Poor's, 2010.
2 Webster & Bishaw, 2007.

national Experian-Gallup survey, published April 18, 2007, showed that 3 in 10 consumers across the country found it difficult to make ends meet.[3] As personal savings in the U.S. dropped to a 74-year low, people's greatest worry was not having enough money for retirement. Real average earnings have seen very little change since 1983, providing little room for optimism.

For those with little savings, static income, or low income, the housing affordability index has been so poor that their quality of life is seriously compromised and their very existence jeopardized. Compare this with the number of people who can realistically offer to buy homes and to millions of citizens who will retire in the next few years and whose pensions are not even secured by the government yet.

All this may be a tell-tale sign that the economy is undergoing profound changes. Consumers' buying power may be unable to sustain the housing sector's woes in the future.

The record low interest rates desperately introduced by the Federal Reserve to stave off a complete meltdown of the overall economy due to astronomical debts amassed by the country in the last ten years or so are continuing to entice buyers to buy into real estate with very small down payments. This is causing prices to inflate to the point of becoming downright unaffordable in relation to average incomes. Even a modest increase in interest rates may bring about profoundly negative changes in the economic climate.

All of this does not bode well for the future. The Great Depression of the 1930s may come to haunt us again and

---

3 Experian-Gallup, 2007.

with a vengeance of hitherto unseen proportions. As the real estate sector accounts for close to one-third of the entire economy, its collapse may cause upheavals among the masses, shaking our society to its very foundation. Governments should waste no time; they should intervene by regulating and tightening mortgage-lending standards and practices. And soon, too, before the situation spins out of control. People of today may not be content to wait placidly in soup lines, homeless and broke, the way people, most of them newly arrived immigrants, did during the Great Depression.

Governments must step in and ensure that today's rampant condominium development, which is creating a major habitat style for citizens of the 21st century, is responsibly regulated and planned. One country that has taken positive action in this respect is China. In 2011 it started to curb rampant speculation by investors, instructing its banks to stop extending mortgages to people buying their third condominiums in the country's major cities.

Speaking of China – and India and Brazil, for that matter – another, far more serious situation could develop as a result of the ever-increasing number of real estate purchases by newly wealthy emerging foreign investors. These buyers may bring temporary relief to the economy as a whole but could cause irreversible damage to American citizens who may not be able to equally compete with those investors in future. Simply put, the bidding on real estate by such wealthy buyers will drive prices out of the reach of what most Americans can afford.

I realize that what I have said about the condo phenomenon and real estate market as a whole is bleak. Frankly, it is meant to be. I hope my words will scare away prospective condo buyers with a weak financial basis for owning a condo. I also hope that the rest of this book will wisen up those who are capable of buying a condo or who already own one. The truth can hurt, but it also can heal.

However, I do end the book on a brighter (though still serious) note by giving specific recommendations – to buyers, existing owners, condo boards, and every institution involved in condominium life – that could help make things a lot better. Chapter 6 of my book examines some of the much-needed reforms to the condo system. Residential ownership can still be viable for many current and future condominium owners, but only if the present structure of ownership undergoes some major and much-needed changes.

CHAPTER 1

The Ten Commandments of
CONDO BUYING

1 DO NOT RUSH

It's human nature to buy on impulse. The young or inexperienced may fall in love with a sharp-looking used car and buy it without giving it a thorough mechanical inspection. Later, when they discover defects that the dealer wasn't aware of or failed to disclose, they learn what it means to have bought a "lemon."

Similarly, an over-eager condo buyer may run into difficulties by signing on the dotted line without thoroughly examining the condominium unit and its complex for potential problems.

Many condo buyers succumb to:

- The promise of the condo lifestyle of carefree living

- The allure of becoming their own landlord

- The pressure of sales pitches which may be unfounded

Being in a rush to buy can obscure important aspects of condo buying. Besides its obvious benefits, condo ownership is also fraught with many perils.

The rest of the commandments provide you with invaluable tips and information while you search the market for a condo unit, but this first commandment, "Do not rush," applies to all of them. You must take time for careful consideration before committing to what is likely to be the biggest investment you'll ever make. Slow down! Otherwise, you may succumb to developers' and/or real estate brokers' commission-driven sales pitches and make an unwise decision.

Don't trust others to make decisions for you. Take your blindfold off and read the commandments with care. By adhering to them, you can develop your own real estate buying skills and take control of your own destiny.

- **DO NOT RUSH INTO BUYING A CONDO**

- **RUSHING MAY LEAD TO OWNING A "LEMON"**

2 BEWARE OF BARGAIN PRICES WITH HIGH MAINTENANCE FEES

If you come across a condo unit that's selling at a rock-bottom bargain price, think twice before signing a contract. Condominium complexes may have no choice but to sell their units for a song – sometimes as low as $25,000 per unit. Because of mismanagement or poor construction, sometimes coupled with a drop in the real estate market, these complexes may have depleted their reserve funds to cover maintenance and repairs. They compensate for low selling prices by charging higher than normal monthly maintenance fees.

In other words, what you save on the price of the unit, you'll end up paying back in higher maintenance costs. Over time, you may find yourself imprisoned in a financially troubled complex with a unit that's nearly impossible to resell.

Many buyers of these "bargains" are driven by the notion that writing a monthly check for higher carrying costs will pay off in the long run once the market turns around. They think that, when they eventually sell their unit, its value will have increased to the point that it will recoup the costs they've racked up in paying those higher maintenance costs.

Unfortunately, it may take months – or, more likely, years – for the market to improve. These unfortunate owners may end up losing money. Worse yet, they may be bombarded by a myriad of ongoing demands from their condo board through special assessments to replenish the reserve fund, service the common loan, and pay for legal fees, etc. Should unit owners be unwilling or unable to meet these demands, the board will place a lien on the units and eventually take them over and sell them – at a bargain price – to the next crop of unsuspecting buyers.

Historically, financially weak condo complexes are prone to being wound down, through voluntary or involuntary bankruptcies.

Bottom line: Beware the marketing schemes of desperate condominium complexes promising better days in the future.

- **STEER CLEAR OF CONDO COMPLEXES THAT OFFER UNITS AT BARGAIN PRICES WITH EXCESSIVELY HIGH MONTHLY MAINTENANCE FEES**

3 BUY AT THE RIGHT TIME

To understand how important it is to buy at the right time, just think of condo units that, only a few years ago, sold at very high prices but lost their value – many of them as much as 50 percent or more – as a result of the American real estate collapse of 2006/07.

For example, brand new units on Brickell Ave. in Miami, which were selling for up to $600,000 before the crash, took a dive in value almost overnight. Some ended up selling at the (relatively) meager price of $250,000, or even less. This same phenomenon occurred in Los Angeles, Denver, Phoenix, Las Vegas, and other urban centers.

Something very similar happened, during the major market crash of 1989/90, to major American urban centers.

There's no question about it: The condo market will be adversely affected again; the only question is when.

At the height of the market, condo units were sold to people who had previously rented apartments. They bought their units with very small down payments. This led other such renters to enter the market. Soon, ownership of the condos was largely composed of previous renters with little or no cash reserves and unstable jobs.

These buyers made their decision innocently, hoping to ride out the real estate bonanza until they could resell their unit at a profit.

In fact, there's always a limit to how high speculative trends can rise, and sure enough, eventually the bonanza ended. The market became saturated with condo units. Owners panicked as the value of units plummeted. As a recourse, they rented their unit out for whatever they could get or walked out.

These unfortunate and former unit owners ended up with a ruined credit record as a result of unpaid bills and judgments due to foreclosures, making them much weaker financially than they were before they bought their condo.

The idea is to buy a condo unit at the right time, but the problem is that no one can predict with any degree of certainty when the right time is. There are, however, some common-sense indicators that you can take into account.

Don't pay too much attention to real estate brokers' forecasts – or, for that matter, to banks' analyses of the markets

– because these prophecies are mostly profit-driven. The real estate brokers' and bank executives' very livelihood depends on boosting consumer confidence. They shouldn't be taken as impartial sources regarding markets.

Instead, pay close attention to official government findings regarding the stability of interest rates for the immediate future and beyond, the surplus of unsold real estate, and the state of the overall economy. Reports of these findings are published in newspapers, broadcast on TV, and posted on the Internet.

In the end, regardless of market conditions, the right time to buy is:

- When you can buy your condo unit at a price that requires no more than one-third of your annual income to cover mortgage payments, maintenance fees, and realty taxes

- When you're able to obtain a mortgage at a very favorable interest rate and lock in for many years to recession-proof yourself from exposure to market swings

The old adage "buy low, sell high" may be followed by exercising common sense, namely, buying when many unsold units are available, when interest rates are set to remain at favorable levels for some time to come, and when there are signs of improvement in the overall economy.

- RELY EXCLUSIVELY ON GOVERNMENT SOURCES REGARDING MARKET CONDITIONS, INTEREST AND UNEMPLOYMENT RATES, AND CONSUMER CONFIDENCE LEVELS

- ALWAYS BUY A CONDO UNIT AT A PRICE THAT REQUIRES NO MORE THAN ONE-THIRD OF YOUR ANNUAL INCOME TO COVER MORTGAGE PAYMENTS, MAINTENANCE FEES, AND REALTY TAXES

- TO ACHIEVE ULTIMATE PEACE OF MIND, GO FOR LONG MORTGAGES WITH A SET INTEREST RATE, SO THAT YOUR OVERALL EXPOSURE REMAINS CONSTANT

- BY ACHIEVING THESE CONDITIONS, YOU WILL AUTOMATICALLY CREATE YOUR OWN "BUY AT THE RIGHT TIME" GOAL. IF YOU ARE IN NO POSITION TO ACHIEVE THESE CONDITIONS, DO NOT RUSH. SAVE AND WAIT UNTIL YOU ARE

4 MAKE A LOW OFFER

Notwithstanding market conditions, always start with a low offer, say, 75 percent of the asking price. Don't feel embarrassed or intimidated by the real estate broker. If the broker doesn't want to present your low offer, find another one who will. If there are multiple offers for the condo unit you're interested in, don't let your broker get you into a bidding war. Walk away and consider another unit.

Before making an offer, check with other local realtors to find out how much the unit would fetch on the open market if offered for sale. Make sure that the monthly maintenance fees are in line with comparable financially sound buildings. Knowing that you're not overpaying for your unit will give you additional peace of mind.

You may think an offer that's so far below the listing price won't stand a chance of succeeding. Not true. As in so much of life, you will eventually succeed if you are persistent. Even during a healthy market, there are unit owners who are in financial difficulty and are looking for a way out. You owe it to yourself to obtain the best possible price for the unit you're shopping for.

Some of the most successful real estate investors routinely search for properties that can be bought for less than the current market commands. These are solid and resalable properties, whether condos or another type of real estate – not to be confused with a bargain-priced, high-maintenance condo, as discussed in Commandment 2.

To succeed in buying a property at below-market prices, you have to monitor available condo units patiently and persistently over time.

Spending time to find a unit at a favorable price may pay good dividends long into the future. Smart real estate investors usually create equity in their unit at the very time of the purchase, realizing increased value right off the bat.

- **ALWAYS PLACE OFFERS SUBSTANTIALLY LOWER THAN THE ASKING PRICE. NEVER BECOME PART OF A BIDDING WAR**

- **BE PATIENT. THE RIGHT OPPORTUNITY WILL PRESENT ITSELF OVER TIME**

- **STRIVE TO CREATE EQUITY RIGHT FROM THE START**

5 BUY WITH A SOLID DOWN PAYMENT

The more money you put down, the lower the mortgage and the greater your ability to refinance it later on.

A solid down payment of at least 25 percent will act as a buffer for you at mortgage-renewal time should interest rates increase or the value of your unit decrease because of a market slowdown. If the market drops in value when it's time for you to renew your mortgage, your only bailout, unless you have cash reserves, will be to apply for a high-ratio mortgage by utilizing whatever equity you might have in your property – from the initial down payment you put into it.

In general, a solid down payment will enable you, in times of trouble, to more safely arrange a new high-ratio mortgage, private financing against your equity, or a line of credit from your bank.

In contrast, if you buy a unit with a small down payment (5 to 10 percent), you may find yourself in a very real predicament down the road for the simple reason that there may not be any equity in your condo unit if the market tanks.

Whatever the size of your down payment, it should never be borrowed. It should come from your own savings, accumulated over time. Borrowing money for a down payment is risky and ill advised. It creates inequity in your budget and could put you in a very precarious position, even compared with those who buy condo units with very little or no down payments.

The immediate benefit derived from making a solid down payment is the reduction, from day one, of the size of your mortgage and the amount of your monthly payment. It minimizes the mortgage insurance premiums compared with what you would pay on a more expensive, high-ratio mortgage. Over the years, expensive mortgage premiums such as these add up to many thousands of dollars.

Here's a cautionary tale about buyers who purchased their unit with small or zero down and relied strictly on their paycheck to look after the monthly carrying costs of the unit. During the early part of 2000 and onward, while the markets were reaching record highs, there were opportunities aplenty for buyers to buy condo units with a small or zero down payment. Some even realized profits. However, the number of these buyers pales compared with the number who became victims of the market slowdown, losing their condo unit and acquiring a bad credit rating.

Speculating in condominiums, even during the best of times, is one of the riskiest businesses in the real estate industry.

Buying any property with little or no down payment is like going to a casino with $20 expecting to gamble all night and end up with a profit.

- **DON'T HAVE A SOLID DOWN PAYMENT? DON'T BUY!**

- **DON'T BORROW MONEY FOR THE DOWN PAYMENT**

- **WAIT TILL YOU'VE SAVED ENOUGH MONEY FOR A SOLID DOWN PAYMENT**

- **THERE WILL ALWAYS BE GREAT OPPORTUNITIES TO BUY A CONDO UNIT. THE LONGER YOU WAIT, THE BETTER YOUR CHOICE OF WHAT TO BUY**

6 BE CAUTIOUS WHEN BUYING DURING PRE-CONSTRUCTION

It may seem a straightforward proposition to buy a condominium unit during pre-construction, often based on architectural drawings at the sales site. However, it is anything but.

Developers often redesign the layout of units as they go, as a result of changes made necessary during construction. Moreover, they draft purchase contracts such that, if they're late in completing the complex, the purchaser is forced to agree to delays or to occupy their unit while the complex is still awaiting the occupancy permits of units that may still be under construction.

Buyers are well advised to consult a lawyer and insert their own conditions into purchase contracts. By specifying a fixed date of completion, they put themselves in a position to get their deposit back should the developer have grossly miscalculated the timing. Shy away from any purchase in which the developer is not willing to accept such conditions; otherwise, you will be putting yourself at the developer's mercy.

Condominium fees are guaranteed only for the first year of operation. Developers often calculate their initial budget on the low end to make condo units more appealing to buyers.

Almost as a rule, in the second or third year after assuming the complex from the developer, unit owners get hit with considerably higher monthly maintenance fees to cover the developer's cost overruns. Buyers should assume and expect that there will be an increase in maintenance fees from the first year onward, following the completion of their new condo complex.

- **WATCH OUT FOR CONTRACTS THAT FORCE YOU TO BUY THE CONDO UNIT EVEN THOUGH CONSTRUCTION IS CONSIDERABLY DELAYED**

- **WHEN BUYING DURING PRE-CONSTRUCTION, COUNT ON HIGHER MAINTENANCE FEES THAN ORIGINALLY CALCULATED BY THE DEVELOPER**

---

7 MAKE SURE YOU CAN AFFORD THE CARRYING COSTS

Don't forget that, aside from your mortgage payments, you're responsible for other carrying costs, which include maintenance fees, realty taxes, and special assessments. Obtain the status certificate of the unit you wish to buy and the condo complex's financial yearly reports. Analyze the current, past, and proposed future budgets of the complex where you wish to buy. Determine whether one-third of your monthly household income will be sufficient to pay monthly costs. Ask your lawyer or accountant to help you if you're unable to make this analysis yourself.

It is pivotally important for you to be able to afford to carry your property comfortably. Your quality of life may be compromised if the total carrying costs exceed more than one-third of your household income. You will likely end up strapped for cash and enslaved by financial obligations that will deprive you of the quality of life every citizen expects. This is especially true for families with young children.

Consider the effect of changing interest rates. Many people forget that, historically, interest rates have fluctuated anywhere from 2 percent at the end of the Second World War all the way to 18 percent in the early 1980s. For most of the 1970s, rates fluctuated between 6 and 12 percent.

Since the real estate crash of the 1990s, interest rates have seldom reached as high as 6 percent. Rates have been kept at almost historical lows to stimulate buyers into buying real estate. An unintended effect of low rates, however, has been the creation of greater demand for real estate, driving prices so high that ownership has become unattainable for most.

Major oversupply and the saturation of real estate products in the U.S. precipitated a major real estate crash by 2006.

It's only a matter of time before inflationary trends drive interest rates upward, making real estate properties even more expensive to carry and therefore less desirable to buy.

All that said, you could argue that an adventurous and courageous single person, or a couple with no immediate plans for children, might in good conscience choose to compromise their quality of life for a period of time, say ten years or so, during which most of their available financial resources, 60 percent or so, are put toward mortgage payments with the goal of paying it off before its maturity.

The choice is ultimately yours, but don't forget that accelerated payments on mortgages usually come with a tradeoff: a loss of quality of life as the bulk of your income is shoveled into your residence.

- ANALYZE YOUR YEARLY INCOME CAREFULLY AND CALCULATE YOUR ABILITY TO COVER THE CARRYING COSTS OF THE PROPERTY

- DON'T GET INTO A SITUATION WHERE MORE THAN ONE-THIRD OF YOUR INCOME WILL HAVE TO GO TOWARD CARRYING COSTS. FOR EXAMPLE, IF YOUR HOUSEHOLD INCOME IS $60,000, YOU CAN ALLOCATE ONLY $20,000 PER YEAR, OR $1,700 PER MONTH, ON YOUR MORTGAGE PAYMENT AND MAINTENANCE COSTS

- IF THE CONDO UNIT YOU'RE LOOKING AT IS TOO EXPENSIVE, JUST WAIT IT OUT. CORRECTIONS OFTEN OCCUR. THE COST OF UNITS WILL EVENTUALLY (AND SOONER THAN LATER) BECOME MORE AFFORDABLE

8 BEWARE OF COMPLEXES WITH MANY UNITS RENTED OUT

Back in the mid-1960s, when condominiums were born, condos were meant to be an affordable alternative to traditional homes. Many renters aspired for better living arrangements and bought a condo.

Over time, particularly from 2000 onward, the construction and sale of condos increased exponentially, fueled by low interest rates. The industry, composed of too many condo units, caused two major economic crashes in recent history, one in 1989/90, which affected the U.S. and Canada, and the other in 2006/08, which affected mainly the U.S. During each crash, the values of condominiums plummeted up to 50 percent or more. Many condo owners experienced a great loss of equity – in fact, many lost their condo units to foreclosure. They couldn't afford them, either because they hadn't made a sufficient down payment or were not financially strong enough to maintain their unit's carrying costs.

As the markets became saturated and condo units became too expensive, the pool of available buyers decreased. The massive fallout of condo owners placed the condo complexes in the precarious position of having too many empty units, which therefore were not contributing to the monthly maintenance dues. The rules had to be relaxed for the complex to survive. The empty units were eventually rented out. Consequently, many complexes became a mixture of condo owner-residents and renters.

In the condo ownership arrangement, all unit owners strive to ensure that the condo complex is run properly, with common element areas kept clean and presentable. Such common care is supposed to create a better quality of life and living conditions compared with ordinary apartment living.

In contrast, a renter doesn't have a personal stake in the ownership of the building and may not be committed to looking after the complex to the same degree as the unit owner. Renters are far more likely to break condo rules regarding noise and upkeep, resulting in the degradation of the complex. A complex that is heavily rented out becomes unappealing to potential buyers.

In fact, many financial institutions judge a condo complex to be risky if more than 25 percent of the units are rented out and therefore refuse financing to new buyers. As a result, such condo complexes may become desperate. To attract buyers, they may start selling the vacant units at bargain prices, adversely affecting the value of the other units. As a complex makes the transition from mostly owner-occupied to mostly rented, it enters a very dangerous stage: it may turn to private financing, known as common loans, to maintain its very existence – passing the costs along to the condo owners, of course.

Avoid such risks by making sure you check the condominium complex thoroughly before you buy. Ascertain how many condo units are being rented out. You can do so by visiting the complex itself and talking to the occupants and owners of condos in the complex.

If 25 percent or more of its units are rented, stay clear of the complex. It very well may have a dark future.

- **DO NOT BUY INTO A CONDO COMPLEX THAT HAS RENTED OUT MORE THAN 25 PERCENT OF ITS UNITS**

- **THE EXCEPTION TO THIS RULE MAY BE CONDO COMPLEXES LOCATED IN TOURIST RESORT AREAS WITH HIGH RENTAL DEMANDS**

9 CHECK THE PHYSICAL FACTS

It's a good idea to get physical before buying. Check a prospective unit carefully, and, even more important, check the condo complex. You'll be glad you spent the time and money on this if a complex you walk away from later proves to have been poorly constructed or mismanaged.

Condominium complexes are not all the same. The complexes are built by different builders. The quality of construction often varies. Find out how old the condominium complex is. If you're considering a new development, look into the builder's reputation and experience.

When buying into an existing complex, find out whether

it has experienced undue or unexpected repair problems in the past or whether there are any anticipated future repairs. Keep in mind that the cost of repairs will eventually come out of your own pocket via special assessments. If the condo complex is older, or is a conversion from a previous rental apartment building, with a history of poor maintenance or frequent repairs, it is more likely to experience problems in the future.

Whether or not you end up using the pool or gym, you'll still have to pay for their upkeep in your monthly maintenance fee. The more amenities available to you, the higher the monthly fees, both today and in the future.

Pay attention to how utilities are billed. If energy costs are billed on an actual per-unit basis, you will have more control over your energy use and monthly costs. Be mindful of the fact that condominiums are going green. Also, consider that many cars will eventually run on electricity. The cost of installing new circuits and plugs in the parking areas of complexes will be passed on to all owners.

To conduct a proper check before financing the unit, be sure to employ a professional home inspector and lawyer.

Whenever possible, make an offer to buy your unit with the closing day set for 90 days and with at least 60 days of conditional or contingency clauses to obtain a satisfactory home inspection report, conduct legal searches, and perform other due-diligence checks. This will ensure that you're not squeezed for time when making your final decision.

Some condominium complexes may be self-managed; others may employ an outside property-management company. If the latter is the case, research the management company's reputation. Inquire whether the condo board members are capable of ensuring that responsible financial stewardship is in place.

Thoroughly check the yearly financial report of the complex and the status certificate of the condo unit you wish to purchase. They should contain: facts relating to financial and management stability of the complex; the most recent audited financial statements; a record of assessments; any pending or anticipated legal actions; anticipated common element repairs; the anticipated common loan; anticipated increases to reserve funds; anticipated structural or mechanical repairs; and municipal work orders.

Insist that any of the above information that is not included in the status certificate or financial report of the complex be given to you in writing. Don't forget that the seller and board should have nothing to hide if the complex is healthy and well managed. The facts they present should be absolutely true. If they deny any access to the facts, then buyer beware! Something must be wrong.

Besides checking the written disclosures, you should visit the complex. Knock on doors and speak to residents to determine the complex's overall well being. Find out if there is any discord among the members of the board or displeasure with the management company. Ask whether there are any other problematic issues with the complex not addressed in the written disclosures. This additional information may prove invaluable to you in making your final decision about buying the unit.

Any serious discord and/or disconnects among board members, such as constant bickering, fighting, or the formation of factions, are usually precursors of mismanagement and lack of proper governance of the condo complex.

Such situations inevitably lead to legal actions between the unit owners and the board, at the expense of all, depleting the common budget.

There are no quick fixes once board members start bickering. Changing the membership of the board is very difficult and tedious. The overwhelming majority of the unit owners have to be called together to form a special meeting aimed at requiring board members to resign.

This is where politicking comes into play in the worst possible way. Practically speaking, it is very difficult to straighten out such situations and restore a state of normalcy.

- **MAKE A LIST OF THE FACTS AND CHECK THEM OUT ALONG WITH YOUR HOME INSPECTOR AND LEGAL EXPERT**

- **THOROUGHLY EXAMINE THE STATUS CERTIFICATE OF THE UNIT YOU ARE CONSIDERING AND THE FINANCIAL YEARLY REPORTS OF THE COMPLEX**

- **ANALYZE POTENTIAL PROBLEMS (READ: EXPENSES)**

- **FIND OUT ANY EXPECTED OR LIKELY FUTURE INCREASES IN MAINTENANCE FEES**

- ASK THE OTHER OWNERS, YOUR HOME INSPECTOR, AND YOUR LAWYER ABOUT ANYTHING THAT THE BOARD DOES NOT WANT TO DISCLOSE THAT MAY NECESSITATE BUDGET OVER-RUNS, SUCH AS WORK ORDERS ISSUED BY THE MUNICIPALITY, CONTEMPLATED LEGAL SUITS BY THE OWNERS AGAINST BOARD MEMBERS, AND POTENTIAL LAWSUITS BY THE CONTRACTORS FOR UNPAID BILLS

- KNOCK ON THE DOORS OF PRESENT UNIT OWNERS BEFORE YOU COMPLETE YOUR PURCHASE. IF YOUR INVESTIGATION UNCOVERS ANY SERIOUS ADVERSE CONDITIONS, WALK AWAY

10 CONSIDER DEMOGRAPHICS AND FUTURE RESALE VALUE

Before buying, acquaint yourself with the neighborhood where the condominium unit is located. Conduct a physical inspection. Find out if there are railroad tracks nearby, heavily traveled roadways, or major power lines. Noise and ground tremors may interfere with the peaceful enjoyment of your unit in the future. Power lines may present potential health hazards. Problems like these make a condo unit much harder to resell.

Check the present, previous, and anticipated future demographics of the area to make sure that you and your children do not end up the victims of crime. Condominium units in high-crime areas pose exceptionally high risks, not only physically but also in decreased real estate value should you decide to resell later on.

Consider location very carefully before you buy your unit. Congested urban areas may be considered desirable, but don't rule out more open suburban areas, where, besides the fact that unit sizes tend to be larger, there are playgrounds for children and opportunities for quality outdoor living.

Condominium units in the suburbs are usually less expensive. Provided that roadways to schools and downtown areas are accessible and public transit is available, there is nothing wrong with locating outside ritzy and expensive urban centers.

Before you buy, carefully consider specific features that will enhance the resale value of your unit. Keep in mind that bachelor and junior bedroom units are harder to sell than one-bedroom units, units with a den, or two-bedroom units. Even single people or childless couples tend to prefer two-bedroom condos because the second bedroom can be used as an office or for guests.

Units located in the vicinity of power lines and busy roadways or railway tracks are less desirable and therefore more difficult to resell. The same is true of units that were bought without a parking space or without an option to buy one. Units with nine-foot ceilings are much more attractive than ones with lower ceilings. The view from the unit is equally important. A unit facing another building across the street will fetch a lower price than one with a clear view of open spaces.

- CHECK THE DEMOGRAPHIC TRENDS – PAST, PRESENT, AND FUTURE – OF THE LOCATION OF THE UNIT YOU ARE CONSIDERING. IS THE AREA IMPROVING OR DETERIORATING? GO OUT, OBSERVE, ASK THE UNIT OWNERS QUESTIONS, AND CHECK WITH THE LOCAL MEDIA. NEVER BUY A UNIT IN A HIGH-CRIME AREA OF YOUR CITY

- IS THE CONDO COMPLEX CLOSE TO POWER LINES, A BUSY ROADWAY, OR RAILWAY TRACKS? ANY OF THESE CONDITIONS WILL MAKE IT HARDER FOR YOU TO SELL YOUR UNIT LATER

- BACHELOR AND JUNIOR ONE-BEDROOM UNITS ARE HARDER TO RESELL

- UNITS WITHOUT A PARKING SPACE ARE HARDER TO RESELL

- UNITS WITH HIGHER CEILINGS ARE MORE APPEALING AND EASIER TO RESELL AT FAVORABLE PRICES

- THE VIEW FROM THE UNIT IS AN EXCEPTIONALLY IMPORTANT RESALE FEATURE

- CHECK WITH THE MUNICIPALITY WHETHER THERE ARE ANY OTHER BUILDINGS SLATED FOR ERECTION IN THE PROXIMITY OF THE COMPLEX, AND WHETHER THEY WILL OBSTRUCT THE VIEW FROM THE UNIT YOU'RE INTERESTED IN BUYING

A WORD OF CAUTION

Many younger unit owners buy their condominium unit as a springboard for purchasing a traditional property. They believe, rightly or wrongly, that proceeds from the future sale of their unit will give them the economic means to move into a house. This may be a good strategy during favorable market conditions, but economic down-turns, accompanied by adverse market conditions marked by high interest rates, render this springboard scenario nothing more than wishful thinking.

Under adverse market conditions, condo unit owners might not be able to readily sell their units at favorable prices. Many would be forced to remain in their units until economic circumstances change for the better. And that could end up being a long wait. Having no other choice, some people could end up raising their family in their unit, which is not as conducive as a traditional home for quality child-rearing.

While it is true that traditional homes require hands-on maintenance and daily chores, don't forget that you're the master of your own home, with no mandatory monthly maintenance fees. If you choose not to repair your roof or cut the grass in your backyard, no one can force you to do so. Condominium ownership does not provide this kind of liberty.

Because of the financial and social diversity of condo complexes' unit owners, there are many unknowns with regard to how well things may turn out for condominiums. Moreover, communal ownership structures such as condominiums contain some very serious, inherent shortcomings and pitfalls.

The pages ahead point out many largely unknown but obvious shortcomings of condominiums and provide unit owners and their board members with invaluable remedial recommendations to improve the viability, safety, and value of the condominium ownership arrangement.

Potential buyers and existing condo unit owners should read the rest of this book carefully to familiarize themselves with the largely unknown problematic issues surrounding condo ownership in order to cope with them more safely in the future.

CHAPTER 2

The Realities of

CONDO LIFE

Communal living arrangements, by which two or more people jointly own real estate, can be traced back to ancient Rome, although some historians argue that such ownership structures existed even earlier. Urban residences in the form of apartment buildings of various types have existed for at least several hundred years. At the beginning of the 20th century, the need to utilize space in congested urban areas prompted developers to construct more apartment units. By the early 1920s, low- and medium-rise apartment buildings were becoming increasingly popular in the North America.

Traditionally, the landlord who rented apartment units to tenants owned the building. Rent was determined by the fundamental economic factors of supply and demand, although landlords took tenants' incomes into account to keep rental rates competitive.

However, tenants who wished to become their own land-lords began buying apartments from landlords. In so doing, tenants collectively became masters of their buildings as opposed to merely guests. Such legally arranged communal arrangements were originally known as cooperatives.

While cooperatives may benefit from the pre-selected level of financial homogeneity of their occupant share-holders, they may nevertheless be tested in the future by the challenges of a volatile economy.

History shows that scores of cooperative buildings were decimated as a direct result of the financial hardship experienced by individual unitholders. Most of these unitholders were the victims of unemployment or ever-increasing financial demands by their cooperative, which was struggling to maintain its building. Aside from the massive crash of the 1930s, numerous cooperatives have since ended up bankrupt, leaving behind a legacy of failure. (See the appendix of this book for more on the history of co-ops.)

Today, condominium owners are ensnared more or less by the same regimented rules and problems associated with cooperatives.

Physically, there is no difference between them. Both espouse a multi-dwelling concept in the form of low-, medium-, and high-rise apartment buildings. The most common form of condominium is an apartment complex, but condos may consist of row townhouses erected on commonly owned land. Condos may also be arranged as stack-up townhouses appearing as a multi-layered development. Similarly, condominium ownership sometimes takes the form of industrial units and offices.

The only major difference between co-ops and condominiums is that a condo unit can be registered in the land registry office by way of an individual proprietary deed. However – and this is where the soundtrack turns serious – such a deed is always subordinate to the common master deed of the whole complex, thereby creating quasi-ownership relative to the individual unit.

You can see that condos share a great deal of DNA with cooperatives.

Most condominium owners are unaware of, or unconcerned about, the shakiness of the condo concept. They wake up to reality only after they buy their unit, especially when the market becomes depressed.

Condominium ownership is often misunderstood as similar, or even identical, to freehold property, but this is not the case. By jointly owning and sharing the common elements of the complex, such as lobbies, recreational rooms, hallways, and common grounds, condominium owners are mandatorily obligated to contribute financially to the upkeep and maintenance of these areas. At the same time, they are subject to the inherent adverse factors of communal ownership, most of them unknown or misunderstood.

Indeed, the very term "condominium" is a contradiction given that it implies both joint ownership and sovereignty.

- Joint means "belonging to or used by two or more"

- Sovereign means having supreme authority, and in this case, the sole mastership of the property

Condominium ownership consists of owning a unit that, physically and legally, belongs to a complex of two or more units plus a pro-rated portion of all common elements in the complex. Therefore, all individual unit owners jointly and indivisibly own the land on which a condominium complex is erected.

The condominium complex, to be registered, is conceived, designed, constructed, approved, and legally organized in accordance with municipal and provincial laws governing condominium existence and use.

All condominiums have one thing in common: individual owners own their actual unit within the complex and jointly own the land on which the condominium complex sits as well as all the common elements: the hallways, entranceways, party rooms, bearing walls, common plumbing, common electrical conduits, roof, garage, swimming pool, tennis courts, landscaped areas, and other amenities.

Following is the basic information you need to know about the legal and practical realities of condos.

THE LEGAL IMPLICATIONS OF CONDO OWNERSHIP

Two-tier Ownership

Most condominium complexes are legally arranged as a condominium corporation. Unlike cooperatives, condominiums are not ordinary corporations. They do not issue capital stock to their shareholders. In fact, condo corporations are governed not by corporation acts but by condominium legislation known by different names such as the Common Interest Ownership Act, Horizontal Property Act, and the Davis-Stirling Common Interest Development Act in California. For the sake of simplicity, this book refers to all such as condominium acts.

Ownership in condominiums consists of a two-tier structure.

- One tier is absolute, pertaining to the individual unit itself

- The other tier is represented by the undivided portion of the pro-rated interest in all common areas including the land underneath the complex

By purchasing a condominium unit, a buyer receives, in addition to the undivided interest in the common elements of the complex, individual ownership, also known as the "deed," of their unit. That deed is, at all times, contingent on and subordinate to the master deed of the common real property, which includes the land and common areas.

Two-tier ownership has many practical and physical challenges. The most obvious is that individual ownership of the unit is always subordinate to the master ownership of the entire complex. This is due to the physical and legal structure of the condominium ownership arrangement. The individual condominium unit occupies space within a complex in which its water supply, electricity, plumbing, and heat are supplied by conduits running throughout the complex. Therefore, the very existence of individual units is dependent on the longevity and physical well being of the entire complex.

Ability to Mortgage: Blessing or Curse?

In legalizing condominium ownership by providing its unit owners with individual deeds, developers and builders were able to persuade financial institutions to lend money to unit owners through mortgages secured by the individual unit deeds.

Financial institutions quickly made good on this opportunity. A mortgage on an individual condominium unit provides them with security in a particular unit, (seemingly) notwithstanding any defaults by other unitholders. As such, financial institutions are in a position to foreclose and dispose of the unit in case of default by the same methods as if they held security in traditional property.

From the communal point of view, mortgages on units provide an added financial protection. If even one individual unit owner defaults on maintenance or special assessment payments, the mortgage holder has no choice but to remedy such a default to safeguard their own interest in the unit.

In real-life scenarios, however, such remedial measures often lead to foreclosures and fire sales. Multiple foreclosures in a relatively short period of time often diminish the value of all of the other units.

Condominium Acts

Condominium acts or other applicable pieces of legislation are responsible for governing condominiums. Since the condominium is still a relatively new real estate product, many provisions of the condominium acts taken for granted today may be affected by court decisions in the future.

Therefore the various acts are mostly guidelines, as many provisions they contain have yet to be tested in the courts.

The ever-increasing demand for more precise legislation means that condominium acts are in constant need of revision. Some versions of these acts are so cumbersome that some legal experts have found it necessary to write guidebooks to explain what they're actually saying. In many instances, even these guidebooks are impervious to comprehension by the average consumer.

Description, Declaration, and Bylaws

For a condominium corporation to be registered under a condominium act, developers must register two basic documents, the Articles of Declaration and the Articles of Description.

The Articles of Declaration and accompanying bylaws provide the foundation for governing and administering the maintenance and repair of common elements. Along with other matters of general administration, these articles and bylaws include:

- The allocation of budgets

- The establishment of the reserve fund and mechanisms for reassessing it

- Fire, extended risk, public liability, and property damage insurance

- A list of issues relating to the use of condominium units

In the early stages of design and construction, the owners of the intended condominium corporation are usually developers or builders. For the condominium complex to be approved and registered, these groups must apply for condominium registration approval. Certain criteria must be met. As far as construction permits go, they are not unlike those necessary to build apartment buildings or other multi-unit housing projects.

The Declaration explains in detail the proportionate share of the common elements attached to each residential unit, proportionate share of the common expenses allocated to each unit, specification of the common elements that may be allocated for the exclusive use of a particular residential unit, the legal description of the real estate property, surveys, engineering and architectural certificates proving that the building has been built in accordance with relevant building codes, and applicable zoning regulations.

The Articles of Declaration include the proposed or already enacted bylaws and rules governing the use of the units and the common elements, management agreement, and insurance trust agreement. The provisions contained in the Declaration and Description form the foundation on which the board of directors acts and the condominium complex is governed.

The Description of the property identifies it in legal terms, including measurements of the land on which the condominium complex is to be erected. The Description also identifies the size of the complex and the number and size of the units and includes a description and measurement of amenities and their intended uses.

As mentioned above, bylaws governing the use of each condominium complex are usually laid down at the beginning by the developer. Later, these bylaws may be expanded, amended, and altered by the condominium's board of directors, provided that the majority of the unit owners agree, and further provided that such changes do not contravene the provisions of the condominium act.

Newly Constructed Condominiums

On completion of the construction of the condominium complex and receipt of the occupancy permit, buyers are often allowed to move in. This can happen before the complex is entirely finished and registered as a condominium. In such a case, the first buyers of a new, pre-registered condominium do not receive ownership of their unit until after the final registration of the condominium corporation. Until such time, the buyers usually pay a "monthly occupancy fee," which is usually equivalent to the monthly interest on the unpaid portion of the sale price, estimated maintenance fees, and estimated portion of the real estate taxes. It is not unusual for the unit buyers of a newly constructed complex to occupy their unit for months or even years before the complex is registered and the buyers legally become unit owners.

Before the final registration and before the sale of at least 50 percent of the units, when the transition of power to the unit owners takes place, some developers may abuse their position. To make the units more attractive, they may simply absorb certain charges for ongoing repairs, maintenance, administrative costs, and management fees. Such practices are short term. Unfortunately, they are quite common and, in fact, unavoidable because during this time the developer controls the board.

There is cause for concern. Montly fees can go up significantly with newly built condos. One accounting firm did audits on more than 200 condominium complexes and found that it was very common to see maintenance fees rise by 40 to 50 percent in year two and another 20 to 30 percent in year three, after the complex had been registered.[4]

To sell their condominium units, developers usually calculate the first year's budget as tightly as possible so maintenance fees appear as attractive as possible to buyers. Buyers are therefore advised that, when buying a brand new condominium, their monthly maintenance fees are likely to increase, often substantially, in the years following the transition of powers from the developer to the individual unit owners.

When developers finally transfer ownership of more than 50 percent of the units within a complex, they reduce themselves to a minority stakeholder and lose their absolute power to govern the condominium complex. At that time, the condominium corporation finally becomes controlled by the individual unit owners through electing their own board of directors.

The provisions contained in the Declaration, Description, and bylaws determine how the board of directors may act. The developer initially drafts the bylaws, which are mostly

---

4 Roseman, 2006.

standard and in line with the majority of condominium corporations.

The Board of Directors

The duties of a board, as a stand-alone entity and through its management arm, include oversight of, and action on, the topics mentioned above: maintenance of common elements, allocation of budgets, setting up of reserve funds, and dealing with various forms of insurance.

The Articles of Declaration and bylaws, once passed, are difficult to change. When the corporation becomes controlled by the individual unit owners, the articles and bylaws can be changed only by a vote of the overwhelming majority of the unit owners, provided that such changes do not contravene the provisions of the condominium act.

Other requirements to register condominium corporations include the qualifications of the developer or builder for new home warranty programs and the payment of applicable fees and levies to the municipal and provincial authorities.

Deposits by individual unit buyers must be kept in trust until registration takes place, usually on finishing construction and receiving the occupancy permits. As well, the drafting of contracts and agreements to purchase individual units in accordance with the prevailing laws of the jurisdiction in which the condominium complex is being built is a prerequisite for registering the condominium.

Full details of the registration process can be found in the condominium acts and corporation acts applicable to the jurisdiction in which the condominium complex is being built. The condominium act is the law; consumers should be reasonably familiar with it before purchasing a condo unit – and seek legal expertise if necessary.

The Condominium Complex

Condominium unit owners feel the obligation and responsibility to maintain their condominium complex – they honestly intend to run it in the most professional and economic fashion. However, problems of finding practical mechanisms to achieve that goal immediately arise, and in many cases persist, given that most unit owners are not professional real estate landlords.

While the condominium units are owned individually, all decisions and responsibilities with respect to the running and governing of a complex – consisting of the common elements and the land on which the condominium is erected – fall on the shoulders of the elected board members who, as a group, may not be business savvy enough to govern their condominium complex in the most professional manner. An inexperienced governing body usually lacks professional effectiveness, leading to mismanagement and costly errors. (See The Necessity of Getting Involved in Board Matters, in the pages ahead.)

THE PRACTICAL IMPLICATIONS OF CONDO OWNERSHIP

Rules and Regulations

The most obvious disadvantage of communal ownership in a condominium complex is living and abiding by the common rules and regulations.

The communal structure of condo ownership dictates that the condominium complex and its use must be subject to rules and regulations by all individual unit owners. These are put in place primarily so occupants in the complex can live in peace and harmony and preserve its value by maintaining its physical well being for the benefit of everyone residing in it.

Each individual condominium unit, therefore, is subject to restrictions enforceable by the common rules governing the occupancy, rental, and enjoyment of the property. Even though individual unit owners may appear to have absolute privacy and unrestricted rights to enjoy their unit, the rest of the property is jointly owned with others. As such, the common rules rigidly limit and restrict an individual owner's rights.

The rules and regulations are usually contained in the condominium documents known as bylaws. Rules tend to be severely restrictive in comparison with living in a traditional home. For example:

- The rules may call for no pets and even no children in some condominium complexes

- The number of occupants residing in an individual unit may be capped

- Operating a home business may be forbidden

- Playing loud music or otherwise making loud noises is likely to be prohibited

Other restrictions may forbid walking in heavy shoes on bare parquet or uncarpeted flooring, storing bicycles on balconies, barbecuing on balconies, decorating or changing the exterior of a unit to the extent that it may not conform to the overall architectural design of the complex, and making interior structural changes. In many cases, renting the unit to others may also be subject to restrictions.

These are just some of the restrictive covenants that are de rigueur when it comes to communal ownership and that may limit individual unit owners' full enjoyment of their abode. The rules are created so the majority of owners can enjoy their unit peacefully in keeping with predetermined standards. They are necessary evils to preserve the value and reputation of the communal complex.

Mandatory Obligation to Maintain

In addition to being obligated to look after the upkeep and maintenance of their respective units, unit owners are financially obligated for the upkeep and maintenance of the common elements by paying a predetermined monthly maintenance fee on a pro-rated basis.

The individual condominium unit owner is only a small part owner in the master deed of the common elements component of the complex, including the land. The final say in running, managing, and determining the budget of the complex is left to the majority of the owners.

The elected board of directors, by majority vote, has absolute power to make decisions regarding every aspect of running and governing a condominium complex. The condominium's original Declaration and its bylaws provide the foundation on which the board administers its governing laws. The major pillar of these laws is a mandatory and constant monthly payment by each unit owner for the upkeep and maintenance of the common elements. An individual unit owner cannot arbitrarily choose not to contribute, even temporarily, to the maintenance of the complex's common elements.

The individual condominium unit owner, who may be compared to a perpetual obligator, is not necessarily bound by the mandatory rule to physically perform the maintenance and repairs, but is bound by an inescapable monthly financial liability to contribute to the maintenance and repairs as determined by the condominium laws.

Given that the individual unit owner's rights are, by and large, subordinate to the communal rules and decisions that may be, in many cases, contrary to the unit owner's own desires, it is debatable whether the term "condominium ownership" is applicable or even appropriate.

The Necessity of Getting Involved in Board Matters

It is logical, then, for unit owners to become personally involved in the electoral process and to keep a keen eye on the condo corporation's board members and their performance. This is an absolute necessity. However, involvement by all unit owners is extremely rare. After all, condos are sold to buyers who believe they can live free from the maintenance and daily chores associated with traditional homes.

Most unit owners lack the professional experience necessary to run a multi-dwelling complex. Many take it for granted that, once they purchase their units, other, more qualified unit owners will be willing to become board members and will cheerfully accept the duties that come along with the responsibilities of governing a condominium complex. Such members, sometimes referred to as "counsels," are expected by all unit owners to work diligently and professionally to assure the best quality of governance of the complex.

The reality, simply put, is different. Newly elected board members consist of unit owners genuinely concerned about the well being of their condominium complex. They nominate themselves to become elected members because they feel they can make the best possible decisions for the benefit of the entire complex. In many jurisdictions, they are expected or even mandated to perform their duties on a voluntary basis or for very low compensation. Regrettably, lack of compensation is often one of the main reasons that things go wrong.

Many newly elected board members, however enthusiastic and caring they may be at the beginning of their mandates, underestimate the scope of their responsibilities and the amount of time needed to diligently govern and run the condominium complex. Over time, they tire out, and their original enthusiasm wanes. They receive very little in return for the time they spend working for others, sometimes not even a simple thank-you, whereas they are the first to receive blame for anything that may go wrong with the complex. Their original commitment often degenerates into indifference and lack of involvement.

There are all too many instances in which such boards, full of resentment and void of expertise in matters of governance, make poor decisions at the expense of the rest of the unit owners.

These boards are ripe for takeover, gradually or all at once, by power-seeking individuals who may have accomplished little in their lives. These individuals often seek an outlet to fulfill their own leadership goals, not infrequently through ill-designed policies. In many cases, the ulterior motives of such individuals may not benefit the complex. In fact, they may work to its detriment. Hence, many boards become divided, consisting of individuals who cannot work together and are unable or unwilling to put the interests of the complex as a whole before their own.

Complexes with a dysfunctional board are de facto run by the outside management company, which often, when it realizes that there is a decision-making problem at the board level, will seize the opportunity to make decisions, often benefiting itself rather than the complex. This may include hiring expensive trades and receiving kickbacks and other perks because the management company knows that a poorly functioning board will be unable to detect, or deter, such nefarious activities, or, worse yet, will not be able to make collective decisions to change the management company.

Just how bad the situation may become is illustrated by a May 25, 2007, *Miami Herald* article in which the founder of the Florida's Cyber Citizens for Justice Organization is quoted as saying that he receives 30 to 50 complaints a day from condominium unit owners who are suspicious of or unhappy with their association's board.[5]

One of the most egregious examples of what can go wrong at the hands of dysfunctional boards and predatory management companies was brought to light in Toronto in September 2011. The head of a property management firm that managed several condominium complexes in the city was accused of misappropriation of up to $20 million, affecting nine complexes with more than a thousand condo owners, who were left on the hook as victims of the alleged fraud.[6]

Individual unit owners become liable for the common loan against their complexes, as will be seen later in this chapter, with the common loan being repaid in instalments by way of "fees" added to the existing monthly maintenance fee.

In the Toronto fraud case, the head of the management firm was able to pass the bylaw in secret by forging board members' signatures to obtain (common) loans against the receivables of the condominium complexes he managed. The monies were then siphoned into the bank accounts of the management company.

---

5 Gehrke-White, 2007.
6 Aulakh & Zlomislic, 2011.

It took six months before the board members realized that a gross impropriety had taken place.

Hence my point about the necessity of becoming personally involved in monitoring the complex. This involves exchanging ideas with neighbors and making sure that only the best and most qualified individuals are appointed to the board. Unit owners must consider, not only their own units, but also the complex as a whole. Attending meetings and actively partaking in decision-making is time well spent. There is simply no other way to preserve the quality and well being of the condominium complex.

Passive owners – who routinely sign proxy papers to allow others to make decisions for them – show no interest in the process of choosing board members and are often left in the dark. They are unaware of who is running the complex; worse yet, by the time they realize that the wrong people have been elected to the board, there is little or nothing they can do to rectify the problem.

But what about those unit owners who do care about what is going on in their complexes? For them to make any changes, they have to assemble a large quorum of unit owners (a quorum is the percentage of owners who must be present for a meeting to be valid) to call for a general meeting of all unitholders to deal with emergency issues at hand. The quorum mandated by the condo's bylaws can be as high as 85 percent.

This process is extremely tedious and time-consuming and seldom results in a quorum. Some unit owners do not live in their units. Others may not be inclined to spend time and energy attending meetings to change something that they consider unimportant.

COMMON ELEMENT COSTS AND THE OPERATING BUDGET

The common element costs, namely the management, maintenance, and repair of the complex, dictate the economics of owning the unit. These costs can strongly influence the condominium corporation's yearly operational budgets and, in the long run, its very survival. Let's examine various common element and maintenance cost factors and the role these factors play in the eventual fate of the complex.

Management costs include the expense of assembling specialists in the field of property management, building trades, maintenance, and security. Other specialists are contracted by the condominium corporation, including insurance agents, accountants, legal counsel, and trade engineers. These specialists all work in concert with a management team to safeguard and maintain the common elements of the complex.

There are obvious costs associated with the upkeep, repair, and management of the complex; hence the need for a common element maintenance fee. Maintenance fees, payable by each unit owner on a monthly basis, vary from one complex to another. Their amount depends on the number of units, the extent of required improvements of common areas, and the age of the complex.

The cost of hiring a management team and the constant need for maintenance, replacements, repairs, and all other chores associated with governing and maintaining the complex all add up to form the overall operating budget jointly funded by the condominium unit owners.

At the beginning of each fiscal year, the board approves the yearly budget, usually based on the previous year's cost history as well as anticipated cost projections for the future. The budget is then approved by the majority of the unit owners and pro-rated proportionally among them. The unit owners are advised of their budgetary obligation vis-à-vis the monthly maintenance fee. The size of the individual condominium unit is usually used as a yardstick to determine the proportionate share of the budget liability allocated to it.

The monthly maintenance fee is composed of the following major common element cost factors:

- Upkeep (maintenance) and repairs

- Management services

- Reserve fund

- Depletion of the reserve fund

- Special assessments

- Cost to remedy poor-quality construction

- Insurance costs

- Accounting and legal services

- Realty taxes

Let's take a brief look at each of these.

Upkeep and Repairs

Upkeep and repairs are the most volatile and unpredict-able component of the condominium common element cost. Even though the fixed monthly maintenance fee for a particular fiscal year may be set in advance, there could be unpleasant surprises for unit buyers later on, should the complex be in need of major repairs.

Throughout the useful life of any condominium complex, inflationary trends will have a constant impact on the costs of upkeep and repairs. The rising cost of building materials, supplies, trades services, electricity, and water, as well as natural gas and oil, where applicable, will inevitably drive the upkeep and repair costs higher, forcing unit owners to pay higher monthly maintenance fees to cover ever-increasing budgets.

During prolonged periods of inflation, when costs of upkeep and repairs outpace the individual unit owner's increase in income, many unit owners will find it increas-ingly difficult to sustain their units.

Uncertainty pertaining to upkeep and repair costs keeps condominium unit owners in a state of suspense. This uncertainty may not play an important role for unit owners residing in newer buildings during times of a sound economy and low interest rates. That could change for them, however, as their complexes age.

Management Services

Good, responsible management is key to the successful operation of a condominium complex. Making sure that the upkeep and repairs are done at the fairest possible prices without compromising the quality of the work, as well as assuring that the common elements of the complex are in a good state of repair and are clean, tidy, and presentable to unit owners and potential buyers, is of paramount importance in preserving the value of condominium units.

Good work by the management company is usually a reflection of a well-functioning board. It is the board's utmost duty to monitor and make sure that the management company does the best possible job in managing and maintaining the complex, while at the same time making sure that any undertakings are cost-effective at all times.

Reserve Fund

The reserve fund is a pool of money set aside for unexpected or unforeseen repairs or any other costs that may occur from time to time that were not accounted for in the budget at the beginning of the fiscal year. The size of the reserve fund varies from one complex to another depending on the size of the complex and its age and state of repair. The size of the most common reserve fund ranges from one-quarter to one-third of the yearly budget allocated for repairs and maintenance of the common elements.

It is not unusual for unit owners' monthly maintenance fees to include a pro-rated portion allocated to the reserve fund. This minimizes the sudden lump sum requests as well as the frequency of special assessment demands to replenish the reserve fund.

The reserve fund is an absolute necessity. It provides the unit owner with an immediate financial buffer from unexpected costs. Without it, the unit owner would be responsible for the full amount of such costs levied against their units at once, which could cause massive financial hardship.

The developer who built the complex usually initiates the reserve fund. Later on, it is pooled from all the unit owners proportionate to their share of ownership interest in the common elements of the complex. New unit buyers usually inherit a portion of the reserve fund by virtue of their unit purchase.

Other than for unexpected or unforeseen emergencies, the reserve fund can be used for any purpose the condominium corporation may choose. This may include:

- Periodic upgrades of common elements

- Replacement of major fixtures, heating, and air conditioning

- Refurbishing or replacing elevators, swimming pools, saunas, and security systems

- Landscaping

Such upgrades are mostly conducted voluntarily, but in many cases they may be also prompted by building and fire inspectors or other relevant authorities.

Reserve funds can be quickly depleted when major repairs of common element areas become necessary. Building and fire inspectors make regular periodic inspections to the complex. In the case of deficiencies or non-compliance, they may issue work order notices to the board's attention. Work orders must be properly attended to within a specified period. They may require immediate action in case of health hazards or emergencies. If they are not acted on within the specified time frame, a fine may be imposed. This fine becomes a charge to all the unit owners.

The municipality has the power to hire outside trades to perform necessary work, in order to guard the safety of the complex, and to charge the cost of such work to the corporation. Before buying a condominium unit, buyers should check with the local municipality for any outstanding work orders against the complex, whether registered or pending.

Condominium corporations keep reserve funds in separate accounts and, in most cases, invest the money in safe securities for the benefit of all the unit owners.

Depletion of the Reserve Fund

As previously noted, sudden and unexpected repairs for which the annual budget has not allocated funds can deplete a reserve fund rapidly. Ongoing compliance with ever-changing building and fire codes often requires spending a portion of the reserve fund.

Condominium complexes that deplete their reserve funds to below the levels required by their own bylaws or as provided by the condominium act must collect additional funds from all the unit owners. This may render the unit owners liable for such additional funds either in lump sums or monthly increments. These charges become due from time to time in addition to existing monthly maintenance fees.

Some well-managed condominium complexes arrange their monthly maintenance fees to include a portion allocated to replenishing the reserve fund to minimize the frequency of special assessments. (See more on special assessments, below.)

It is often difficult to establish what an appropriately safe and adequate reserve fund should be for a particular complex. Some experts suggest that it should be in the range of 20 to 75 percent of the yearly budget, depending on the expected likelihood of major breakdowns and repairs. Most condominium acts stipulate minimum levels for reserve funds that condominium complexes must maintain at all times.

Special Assessments

Special assessments may be levied from time to time against the unit owners to replenish the reserve fund or carry out immediate, mostly unexpected, repairs or replacements to common elements. These assessments heave into view when the reserve fund is low and in urgent need of replenishment. As the complex ages, the assessments tend to become more frequent and substantial. They may arise due to sudden and unexpected damage to the complex, heating elements, electrical conduits, roof, balconies, and facades.

Most repairs are performed voluntarily, either by decisions of the majority or through their board of directors, depending on the size and cost of the repairs. In some situations, however, the repairs must be made involuntarily and contrary to the wishes of the majority. Involuntary assessments may include the cost of an unexpected repair of the roof and replacements or upgrades to various mechanical and structural components as dictated by work orders from municipal authorities.

There is very little that unit owners can do about these orders other than comply. Otherwise, the complex would be in contravention of the existing laws. When the cost of repairs becomes unusually high, with no ability to collect it from the unit owners immediately, the condominium corporation may be forced to obtain a common loan. Such a loan is usually secured against the corporation's receivables. The pro-rated increment of money needed to service such a common loan is an automatic financial liability to all the unit owners and is usually added to the monthly maintenance fee.

Cost to Remedy Poor-quality Construction

This cost forms a part of the special assessment. Unit owners often suffer adverse financial situations if their complex was poorly built. Repair bills can run into the hundreds of thousands, if not millions, of dollars. Individual unit owners could incur five- or even six-figure common element repair bills.

Shoddy construction can take a huge toll on owners. According to media reports, tens of thousands of families continue to suffer emotionally, financially, and physically, having lived for years with leaks, rot, and mold in their homes, as a result of poor construction. In the case of many of these buildings, water penetrated the building envelopes and the moisture inside the units created toxic mold.[7]

There is a very large number of sub-standard condominium complexes across North America. There are many exceptions, but developers are generally driven to obtain maximum profit in the shortest time possible. Therefore they often cut corners in constructing buildings, giving rise, later on, to damages due to poor workmanship. Subsequent remedial and legal action costs translate into special assessments reflected in higher monthly maintenance fees.

Insurance Costs

Insurance is an important factor in the overall common element cost and it is increasingly important as the complex ages. Insurance rates are usually related to the age of the complex, its state of repair, previous claims, and anticipated future claims. Insurance companies constantly pressure governmental regulatory authorities to raise premiums due to the escalation of claims and other risks facing the condominium industry.

For example, in February 1995, a New York–based rating organization asked the Department of Insurance for a 30 percent increase in key components for use in calculating property insurance rates. Over two-thirds of the property insurance market relies on the rating organization's data.

Condominium complexes are adversely affected when such increases are granted. Escalating insurance premiums force boards to increase assessment and maintenance fees. Considerable increases in insurance premiums are not

---

7 Aaron, 2006.

unusual. Back in the 1980s, the cost of liability insurance skyrocketed to unprecedented levels, causing a major dent in communal ownership budgets. As reported by the *Miami Herald* in June 2006, five major insurers in South Florida requested double-digit rate hikes, with one insurer seeking hikes of more than 72 percent.[8]

As yet another example, one homeowners' association in the same part of the state saw its premiums jump to more than $700,000 from $345,000 the previous year. Because of the bigger insurance bill, the homeowners' association assessed each unit owner for $5,000. Even though such insurance rate hikes may be extreme and reserved for areas prone to hurricanes and floods, insurance hikes are certainly expected to rise in the future due to an increasing number of claims and their associated costs.

Any shared-ownership format requires a comprehensive insurance package to protect the unit owners from unexpected losses to common element areas. In most cases, this means that general liability insurance and "all hazards" protection is required. Such insurance relates to all commonly owned property and does not include individual units. Each unit owner, therefore, should have separate insurance coverage.

These all-hazards clauses protect the complex from fire and damages due to high winds. Natural disasters such as floods and earthquakes are usually not included unless specifically requested. Such added coverage may result in severe premium increases depending on where the complex is located.

---

8 Garcia, 2006.

Insurance polices do not cover inevitable wear and tear. As complexes age, repairs and replacements become increasingly necessary. The ever-changing fire and building codes, requiring mandatory replacements of, or upgrades to, outdated equipment, will also contribute to the overall cost of upkeep and maintenance.

Failure to comply with fire codes and other building codes as they are periodically changed and upgraded could result in higher premiums due to the heightened risk. Worse still, there could be outright cancellation due to non-compliance. Eventually there will come a point when repairing or replacing obsolete equipment and/or paying prohibitively high insurance premiums simply becomes unfeasible. This applies to older complexes nearing the end of their useful lifespan.

Accounting and Legal Services

Under normal circumstances, when the condominium complex is kept in a good state of repair and management is performing diligently, accounting and legal costs are usually contained within the limits allocated in the budget.

Problems with runaway legal and accounting costs usually begin to occur when outside trades are not paid on time, causing them to commence legal action for the unpaid bills. In certain instances, unit owners may take legal action against the corporation or its board members for their neglect and unwillingness to look after damages caused to their units.

Such legal claims can escalate, especially when the

grievances of many unit owners lead to multiple legal actions. Costs associated with such actions may become considerable and impact the monthly maintenance fees as an added financial burden to all the unit owners.

As a rule, condo buyers hardly ever consider the legal costs associated with the day-to-day running of the condominium complex. Ignoring these costs can come at a price. Legal costs may come to comprise a considerable portion of the common liability as a result of legal actions of many different kinds.

Some legal costs arise out of owners' disputes pertaining to damages to their units caused by other unit owners. There are many other possible causes of dispute, such as when unit owners decide to challenge their board's competence for non-performance or poor governance. The cost of any legal battle involving the condominium complex is borne by all individual owners in the complex. Money for the corporation's legal or arbitration fees comes from the common budget.

From time to time, local and higher levels of government may commence legal actions for non-compliance with applicable municipal ordinances or provisions of the condominium act.

As the complex ages, legal claims and liens brought against the condominium complex by trades, suppliers, and creditors may become substantial, thereby further denting the condominium's common budget and requiring additional funds to replenish its reserve funds.

Realty Taxes

Realty, or property, taxes are not part of monthly maintenance fees but often are required to be paid on a monthly
basis along with maintenance fees. Taxes are assessed and
levied by the local municipality on every individual condominium unit as a separate obligation. Taxes vary from one
municipality to another and are assessed based on the value,
size, and location of the complex. Taxes fluctuate yearly,
but, in general, they range from 0.5 to 2.6 percent of a unit's
purchase price.

Municipal bureaucrats discovered a convenient new
source of revenue when they created the condominium
unit's separate proprietary deed. They assess individual units
rather than, as in the case of rental apartment buildings, the
whole complex. The resulting taxes, which fluctuate from one
year to another, become the obligation of each unit owner.
Municipalities should not be allowed to unfairly impose
higher taxes on individual condominium units; however,
any changes to policies in that respect are unlikely to occur
anytime soon. Today's condominium unit owners have not
yet formed political lobbies strong enough to change government policies regarding property taxes.

Even cooperative owners are better off. They hold shares
in the cooperative corporation and thus are treated as business asset owners and viewed by municipalities as tenants.

In many cases, cash-strapped municipalities assess individual condominium owners with unfairly high realty taxes
compared with traditional rental apartment buildings in the
same area, even though, physically speaking, they are very

much alike. Such unfair treatment will likely continue as long as condominium owners remain complacent about it. Isolated attempts by unit owners to appeal realty tax rates seldom succeed.

The escalation in realty taxes will continue to be a burden on individual unit owners.

LONGER-TERM ADVERSE ISSUES

Choosing the Lifespan of the Unit

Traditional homeowners have a choice to terminate the lifespan of their house at any time and for whatever reason. They may decide the house is too old or beyond repair and, as such, raze it and build a new one. Or they may decide to sell off the land so it can be developed by someone else.

Owners in a communal ownership setting do not enjoy the same privilege. Their only recourse is to sell their individual unit. To terminate the unit and the complex in which they live, the communal owner would have to convince the majority of fellow unit owners to do the same. Needless to say, this would be an arduous process. In communal ownership arrangements, the majority rules. That majority can often hold opinions contrary to that of individual unit owners.

The same is true when it comes to the individual unit owner's desire to make structural changes to their unit. Any changes, whether of a physical or legal nature, are not within the unit owner's sole discretion but are subject to the mercy of the majority of the unit owners.

Eventually, when escalating costs of repairing and

maintaining a downtrodden common property no longer make financial sense, the unit owners may be forced to wind their complex down. The problem again is one of practicality. Reaching a collective decision to wind down a complex is often very difficult. Some owners, despite escalating costs and the opinions of professional engineers that the complex is no longer sound, may prefer to put the whole complex up for sale to cash in on whatever equity might remain in their real estate. Others may insist on carrying out repairs, clinging to the hope that a future upswing in the real estate market will bail them out.

When owners fail to agree, the communal ownership simply runs out of money and becomes subjected to a winding-down process, usually via bankruptcy proceedings by the complex's creditors.

Default of One Affecting Another

Problems occur when the economy becomes stagnant or goes into a recession, characterized by higher levels of unemployment and/or inflation accompanied by high interest rates. During such times, financially weaker unit owners are particularly prone to default on their obligations. The arrears accumulated due to defaults, despite being secured by a lien placed on the defaulted units by the corporation, become an added financial burden on other unit owners until the defaulted units are sold and the monies due are recouped from the proceeds of their sale.

You may think that, because each condominium unit is deeded separately, a default by one or more unit owners will not adversely affect others. The unfortunate reality is that all unit owners are affected by the defaults of others. This becomes evident when a mortgage holder moves in to claim a defaulted unit through power of sale or foreclosure. Once in possession, such units are sold at public sale or auctions, or through other foreclosure methods, to recoup as much of their investment as possible. The sale price for foreclosed units depends entirely on prevailing market conditions.

When real estate markets are favorable, defaulted units may sell at fair market prices. However, if the market is depressed, mortgage holders, such as banks, seldom have the patience to await a market rebound. Most are not in the business of owning real estate. Their paramount goal is to sell defaulted units at the best possible price in order to recover as much of their investment as possible. This often means selling these units at a loss, as they may not even fetch the price necessary to recover the principal amount of the mortgage.

Such "distress" or "fire" sales automatically impact the values of other units in the complex because all sales are recorded. New buyers will expect to purchase other units within the complex for the same deflated price. In such situations, non-distressed unit owners must wait for market conditions to improve to be able to sell their units at the right price.

Keep in mind that mortgage holders seldom, before such units are actually sold, step into the shoes of the defaulted unit owner to look after accumulated arrears on the monthly obligation of common element and assessment fees. Most mortgage holders are exclusively financial institutions, not obligated to contribute to maintenance fees and other dues on behalf of the indebted unit owner. The lack of contribution to maintenance fees on such defaulted units creates greater pressure on the rest of the owners to replenish the reserve fund for the common budget necessary to maintain the complex as a whole.

Failure on the payment of common element fees is often accompanied by failure of mortgage payments; in fact, the former often triggers the latter. Upon default, mortgage holders begin power-of-sale or foreclosure proceedings to sell defaulted units as soon as possible. Once in possession of defaulted units, mortgage holders generally let the arrears of common element fees and assessments accumulate. The condominium corporation gets paid only when the defaulted unit is sold.

During times of default by some and, in certain cases, many unit owners, the rest of the non-defaulting unit owners shoulder the commonly shared debt. They are forced to wait until the defaulted units are sold before the corporation can recuperate the accumulated debts of defaulted units from the sale proceeds.

In the meantime, should the corporation's budget become depleted, non-defaulting unit owners have to jointly contribute for its replenishment. The common expenses to look after the condominium complex remain the same, notwithstanding how many unit owners pay or do not pay their monthly obligation on time.

In practical terms, the unwillingness of most mortgage holders to stand in for defaulting unit owners and pay off arrears of common element debt and contribute to monthly dues may lead to the rapid depletion of the common reserve fund. The burden of replenishing depleted reserve funds rests on the shoulders of the remaining owners for as long as the defaulted units remain unsold. The condominium corporation may eventually experience financial strain and have to borrow monies from outside sources to stay afloat.

This problem of defaults may become particularly acute when there are no immediate buyers willing to purchase defaulted units, especially during prolonged adverse economic and market conditions. A chain reaction can take place in which owners who previously had financial means begin to crumble under the weight of the accumulated debts of others. To maintain their basic operating budgets, condo corporations may have no other choice but to obtain an outside common loan or offer their defaulted and vacant units for sale at heavily reduced prices just to recover the accumulated common element debts.

I once witnessed, first-hand, numerous blocks of "ghost affected" defaulted units at the beginning of the 1990s, marking one of the major real estate recessions in the U.S. and Canada.

From 1991 to 1995, certain Fort Lauderdale and Miami condominiums were up for grabs at $25,000 to $30,000 in complexes where units previously sold for over $100,000. In other urban centers, numerous condominium units, previously selling for $120,000 to $160,000, were selling in the $40,000 to $60,000 range – in many cases at prices just sufficient to cover the outstanding common debt on receivables, liens, and realty taxes. The same scenario, except for the inflated dollar figures, that occurred during the severe American real estate crash of 2006/7.

In other urban centers, numerous condominium units, previously selling for $120,000 to $160,000, were selling in the $40,000 to $60,000 range – in many cases at prices just sufficient to cover the outstanding common debt on receivables, liens, and realty taxes.

Co-op and condominium units in Manhattan that sold in the $150,000 to $200,000 range in 1990 had been worth close to half a million dollars only a few years earlier. Needless to say, low prices adversely affected the values of other units as well. Condominium corporations and co-op corporations struggled to meet their operating budgets. Widespread defaults were so common in those days that New York City had to place a moratorium on realty tax increases.

Borrowing on Receivables: The Common Loan

Many condominium buyers do not know that their condominium corporation is entitled to borrow money against its receivables when such needs arise.

The necessity of obtaining a common loan is one of the most dreaded situations that an individual condominium owner may experience. Such loans are desperate measures taken as a result of individual owners being unable to carry on with necessary expenditures to maintain the condominium complex. The need for a sizeable common loan may bring serious consequences, forcing out many condominium unit owners.

The necessity of spreading assessment payments out over time, so that the unit owners' monthly obligation becomes affordable, may force the condominium corporation to borrow money from outside finance companies, pledging receivables such as the special assessment fees as collateral.

Loans by condominium corporations create a common financial liability. The common loan may be amortized over several years until it is fully paid. When some owners are unable to regularly contribute their pro-rated share to service the common loan, more pressure is put on other, non-defaulting unit owners, who are left with no choice but to make up for the difference from the reserve funds. A rapid depletion of the reserve fund puts a further demand on unit owners to replenish it.

Any common loan taken out by the corporation de facto lessens an individual owner's equity in the unit. If the pro-rated share is not paid on time by the unit owner, the corporation may place a lien on the unit, leading to an automatic default under the mortgage. If more than 10 percent of unit owners become unable to meet their monthly obligations to service the common loan, the corporation may go into default. The lender of the common loan may then decide to sue the corporation and subsequently obtain judgements enabling them to start legal proceedings against all defaulting units and the corporation itself.

To make matters worse, the placement of liens on defaulting units triggers mortgages on those units to automatically default, enabling mortgage holders to use the remedy of foreclosure.

This vicious cycle is created by the fact that the mortgage holder's position becomes compromised by the added encumbrance of a lien or charge on the condominium unit, rating in priority to their mortgage. Therefore, a pro-rated portion of the common loan secured against the assessment (and/or other common receivables), even though not originally secured by the condominium units, rates de facto in priority over the mortgages on individual units.

In the case of a depressed economy and high unemployment, financial pressures on unit owners may create a domino effect, causing even more unit owners to default and, consequently, move from or lose their units. The added large liability placed on the shoulders of the remaining unit owners may, in extreme circumstances, become a threat to the very existence of the condominium complex.

Distressed complexes with large common debts may become easy prey for professional speculators who buy defaulted units in blocks, usually at heavily discounted prices from banks and other lenders that advanced the common loans to the complexes.

To avoid such gloomy scenarios, all condominium unit owners must participate in deciding the extent to which their complexes may become indebted, if at all.

Speculative Takeovers

"Unfriendly takeovers" occur all the time in the corporate world. There is no reason to assume that the same cannot happen to condominium complexes, which are mostly arranged as condominium corporations. While takeovers in the corporate world involve shares or capital stock, take-overs in the condominium world involve buying as many distressed condominium units as possible and then gaining control of the board. The successful party or parties, once they are in a position of control, may decide to further their own business agendas, which may not necessarily be in the best interests of the remaining traditional unit owners. In fact, takeovers may turn "unfriendly," with the new controlling unit owners working to the detriment of the remaining unit owners.

Major banks and financial institutions are not the only mortgage holders of condominium units. Others may be private individuals or investment syndicates that were either primary lenders or bought the interest of the mortgage loans from the original mortgage lenders. When in a position to foreclose on defaulted units, such "mortgagees in possession" who, especially during depressed markets, are unable to sell the units at their desired price, may elect to hold on to foreclosed units until market conditions improve.

This may initially seem beneficial for the complex if these new owners contribute regularly to the maintenance and upkeep of their repossessed units. The real problem occurs when a significant number of traditional unit owners default, resulting in an increased number of this new type of mortgage holders in possession. This may have a profoundly negative effect on the remaining unit owners.

Whereas the complex was previously predominantly owned by traditional unit owners who bought their units as their own residences, the complex can now become mixed with non-traditional owners – namely, speculative mortgage holders – who rent their units to minimize their exposure and maximize their financial returns. Eventually, the whole complex may end up resembling an ordinary apartment building rather than a condominium complex. If market conditions remain unfavorable for an extended period, more and more of these types of mortgage holders may take over defaulted units, thereby creating a dangerous level of financial inequity within the complex.

By outnumbering traditional owners, mortgage holders in possession become in position to choose their own board of directors. Once in control, they can dictate their own business agendas, including speculative schemes to facilitate further hostile takeovers.

When in position to dictate the future of the complex they control, these new, financially superior speculative owners may act together to make swift recommendations for (unnecessary) major improvements by levying consider-able assessment fees on individual units and then borrowing large sums of monies against the complex's receivables to carry on with major improvements. All the while they know full well that the traditional unit owners may not be able to afford the repayment on such loans through their increased maintenance fees.

Sudden and often unaffordable assessments and/or an obligation to pay off exceptionally large common debt on receivables may prove disastrous to traditional unit owners, causing them to succumb to condominium creditors or mortgage lenders. Even the strongest of traditional unit owners may have no choice but to relinquish their assets to those who are financially strongest and in control of the complex.

This gives entities controlling such beleaguered complexes the legal right to obtain a court-appointed order to wind down the condominium corporation. The speculators' ultimate goal is to seize the complex and buy it back from creditors and trustees at a considerably lower price. This maximizes their substantial writeoffs against "losses" but, more importantly, it provides them with an opportunity to create significant gains from the future sale of the individual units that were taken over.

The above scenario could be likened to a poker game that involves the hidden agendas of financially strong mortgage-holders in possession of units facing traditional unit owners. The player with the most money can raise the stakes so high that the ordinary player or traditional unit owner cannot stay in the game. At the expense of traditional unit owners, the speculative mortgage holders, through their associated or friendly creditors, may enrich themselves by selling foreclosed units to new buyers or the entire condominium complex to a developer. When the economy is down for an extended period, multiple foreclosures by mortgage holders and the possibility of subsequent takeovers may become one of the most notable disadvantages of owning a condominium.

The corporate experience shows that few or no alternatives are left for the traditional unit owner once the complex is either controlled or taken over by such outside mortgage holders-turned-speculators and/or their related creditors.

From the original residential unit owners' perspective, such a sinister yet legal process may render them without recourse. Faced with considerable losses, they may be forced to move out even before the complex is wound down.

Takeovers are extreme scenarios that may occur during prolonged economic recessions. They can adversely affect condominium ownership and essentially lead to a unit owner's demise. A depressed economy, poor condominium governance, failure to cap or regulate the assignment of receivables to obtain a common loan, and the very structure of condominium ownership can all give rise to serious adversarial situations.

Depreciation vs. Stability of Land

Any construction on land, such as a house or condominium complex and, for that matter, any dwelling constructed of today's materials, has a finite lifespan. These buildings cannot be expected to last forever. There are certain buildings in Europe that are centuries old, some dating back to medieval times. However, if still habitable, they have likely been reinforced, renovated, or retrofitted several times over. To do this to an old structure is often more expensive than to build a new one.

Anything built above ground depreciates over time, due to inevitable wear and tear. Replacements and renovations require capital expenditures that directly impact the pocketbook of the owner.

On the other hand, the land beneath any structure is there to stay, notwithstanding the passage of time or fluctuations due to changes in the economy. The only expense to the land-owner is a realty tax. This tax is omnipresent and unavoidable but typically represents the smallest of all expenses associated with owning any real estate. In the end, the land will provide the owner with the only true value or equity in his or her real estate property.

Land does not physically depreciate due to wear and tear, but its monetary value may vary in accordance with prevailing market conditions governed by the principle of supply and demand.

There are concerns even in the most favorable scenario, for example, when condominium unit owners in old, used-up complexes are living harmoniously. They may make sound and responsible decisions for the future of their complex, such as agreeing to eventually terminate its existence by selling it for the value of the commonly owned land. The end result, however, may not be as advantageous to an individual condominium owner in comparison with a traditional property owner. When divided among all unit owners, the individual proceeds from the land sale of the complex are likely to be considerably smaller in comparison with the proceeds of a traditional property. Unquestionably, this situation is one of the major drawbacks of owning a condominium in the long run.

Financial Disparity and Its Consequences

Financial disparity between individuals is prevalent in any society, and the same is true of communal ownership arrangements like condominiums. There will always be those who are financially better off and are able to regularly contribute to the reserve fund and special assessments and others who may find it difficult or impossible to do so.

During favorable economic times, when unemployment and interest rates are low, financially weaker unit owners are usually able to sustain themselves and meet their financial obligations. In many cases, they may even sell their units for profit, especially during times of high demand. As long as real demand lasts and the economy remains strong, a seemingly homogeneous financial ownership structure may be adequate to maintain the entire complex trouble-free.

Paradoxically, substantial financial disparity among real estate owners may manifest itself in a new and completely unforeseen form.

Since prices of U.S. real estate may be low and attractive to wealthy foreign-born buyers, it will be only a matter of time before Americans experience the consequences of East Asian and South American investors' thirst to buy as much residential property as possible.

This may be a blessing in the short run, as the American economy continues to stumble under its massive internal deficit. However, foreign buyers of American residential real estate and agricultural land may eventually put real estate prices out of the reach of average Americans. This could gravely affect the country's culture and traditions. Economically speaking, it may subordinate traditional U.S. citizens to foreign landlords, transforming the American way of life and its demographic landscape forever.

The time has come for the federal and state governments

to recognize this potential threat and implement radical measures to curb or cap foreign residential real estate investors and speculators, preventing them from taking control of domestic residential real estate.

CHAPTER 3

Owning a Condo
vs. Owning a House

When buying real estate property, whether a condominium unit or traditional home, the most important considerations are price, physical improvements of the premises, and location. These factors, along with demand, determine value.

When the value of traditional property is compared with the value of a condominium unit, a major consideration, in both cases, is the portion of the price allocated to the land.

The land beneath and surrounding the condominium complex is commonly owned. When developers originally purchase a site, the value is determined by its zoning for multi-unit use – most notably, how many units can be constructed. Depending on the location, a developer may buy condominium-approved land for 5 to 15 percent (or more) of the value of each unit they can build on the site.

Land prices for traditional properties vary depending on the size and location of the lot. The land value of traditional property comprises a larger amount, anywhere from 25 to 35 percent (or more) of its total price.

Compare a traditional home with a condominium unit of similar size (for example, a two-bedroom, 1,500-square-foot traditional home valued at $300,000 with a two-bedroom, 1,500-square-foot condominium unit also valued at $300,000). The land value of the traditional home could range from $75,000 to over $100,000, whereas the value of the condominium land would range, on average, from $15,000 to $45,000.

From this perspective, traditional homeowners are automatically better off because of the value and size of their lot. As a rule, the size, and therefore the value, of the traditional homeowner's lot is larger than the undivided portion of the common land belonging to an individual condominium unit owner, even in the pricy downtown core of major urban centers.

As noted before, unlike land belonging to traditional property, the condominium land value cannot be individually and separately claimed, sold, or financed. Sale of the commonly owned land can occur only if approved by the majority of the unit owners in the complex.

Therefore a traditional homeowner is always better off in terms of cashing in on the equity in his land. Homeowners can sell their property, even if the house is in complete disrepair, for the fair value of the land without having to get anybody's permission to do so.

Many of the more expensive condominium units are of equal or larger size than ordinary traditional homes. Additional factors that determine a condo's value include the quality of construction, the extent of amenities inside the complex, the view from the unit, and the location of the complex in the community. To attempt a direct comparison of values between a condominium unit and a traditional property based on the inside amenities would be unfair and, in most cases, incorrect, as one of the most important factors of the equation continues to be location.

You cannot quite compare the value of a condominium unit in upscale urban areas such as Manhattan or Miami with a traditional house of similar size on a standard-size lot in a suburban area. Given the same location, however, you can compare the same size of condominium with the same size of traditional property. Very often, traditional properties in the same area are more expensive, though this may change soon as condominium units continue to gain in popularity.

Some condominiums have obvious advantages over traditional properties. They may be located in desirable, close-to-work downtown locations with elaborate outside amenities such as theatres, shopping malls, museums, libraries, and dining establishments. These amenities, especially if they are within walking distance of the condominium complex, provide an advantage and, therefore, an added measurable value over traditional homeownership. Traditional properties are more likely to be located in the suburbs, often costing their owners time and money spent commuting to work or traveling downtown for other reasons.

Comparison of Maintenance Costs and Repairs

Both traditional homes and condominium complexes require maintenance and repairs; the fundamental difference between them, however, is the fact that traditional homeowners, being true masters of their property, can choose when, and to what degree, to maintain and repair their property.

Lawn care and maintenance of the exterior of the house are entirely at their discretion. If traditional property owners find themselves in financial difficulty, they may not be able to afford to maintain their property as diligently as they would under normal circumstances. They may have no other choice but to leave their property in a state of disrepair or neglect for some time until their fortunes change. This does not put them at risk of losing their home. Owners of a condo unit, in contrast, are likely to lose their property if they fail to keep up with mandatory monthly maintenance fees.

This reveals one of the most profound differences between traditional homes and condominiums. Traditional property owners have a chance to hang on to their property even when they are unable to look after its maintenance and repair. They can decide how to maintain the property without the influence of their neighbors. Only traditional property can provide such ownership.

The condominium owner, on the other hand, is stuck with a predetermined and omnipresent mandatory monthly maintenance fee, set by the condominium corporation, over which he or she has very little control individually.

As for the actual cost of maintenance, it would be wrong to assume that it is more expensive to maintain traditional property than a condominium unit. For the sake of simplicity, assume that the monthly maintenance fee for a two-bedroom condominium unit is $350. You could argue that a traditional home of comparable size would likely cost the same or less to maintain. While grass has to be cut and snow shoveled, the most notable concerns are the costs of paying for the outside porch lights, the surcharge on garbage disposal in some areas and, over time, replacing the roof. Overall, the outside maintenance of traditional property may be cheaper than the pro-rated cost of maintaining the condominium common elements.

Moreover, rather than contracting the maintenance chores out to someone else, traditional homeowners can perform them themselves, thereby reducing their overall costs, albeit at the expense of their own time and labor. Condominium unit owners do not have such a choice.

Affordability Index:
How Much Can You Afford to Carry?

It is worth drilling down on this issue of the affordability of housing vs. condos, by looking more closely at ownership affordability, whether for owning a condo or a house. The ownership affordability index measures the ability of an average family to afford the mortgage on a given property. This chapter reaffirms the "living standards index," namely, that housing costs should be no more than 28 to 33 percent of yearly, pre-tax household income. "Housing costs" includes mortgage payment, utility costs, maintenance fees, and taxes. It also discusses the effect on affordability of real estate prices, the cost of borrowing, and the cost factors that are unique to condominium living.

Typically, banks will not lend mortgage money if the consumer's income is too low to meet this measure.

For example, if a pre-tax household income is $60,000, the bank would usually consider up to 33 percent of such income, equaling $20,000 or so, to be used to service mortgage payments, management fees, utilities, and taxes. At favorable interest rates, let's say 5 percent per year, $20,000 could cover a yearly payment on a $300,000 standard mortgage. The standard mortgage in this case includes the payment of both the principal and interest amortized over 25 years. However, if interest rates rose, say to 8 percent, then that same $20,000 would be able to cover a yearly payment on the same standard mortgage of only $220,000 or so. The difference amounts to a considerable drop of $80,000.

Interest rates, along with household income, dictate the size of the mortgage you can afford to carry. Having sufficient equity or cash reserves increases your ability to survive the upward shift of interest rates.

This is especially true of condominium owners who have not put substantial down payments on their units, have little or no cash in the bank, and can barely keep up with monthly obligations even during favorable economic times. A sudden upward shift in interest rates at the time their mortgages come due for renewal may spell disastrous results for many such unitholders particularly if combined with other previously discussed realities affecting condominium ownership.

The safest way to buy real estate and preserve the roof over your head is to acquire it at a price that you can reasonably expect to carry in terms of obligations, such as mortgage, tax, utility, and maintenance payments. A prudent way to buy real estate is one that calls for at least 25 percent saved cash for down payment, and 33 percent or less of household income for repayment of the mortgage and its related carrying costs. Owners who adhere to this policy can expect to stand a better chance against a slowing economy and increasing interest rates.

Don't forget that a down payment of 25 percent (or in the case of condominiums, even 35 percent) is required to qualify for a mortgage. Buyers would be well served to save adequately for their down payments rather than accept unreasonable risk by obtaining a high-ratio mortgage (usually up to 90 percent of the property value). When the mortgage comes up for renewal, the property may have declined in value due to a slowing market, or interest rates may have risen. By making the normal down payment as suggested above, owners may still bail themselves out by going for high-ratio refinancing. Owners who started with a high-ratio mortgage may end up facing problems – such as not being able to renew their mortgage, or having to stretch their budget over the limit if interest rates increase.

Buyers should not assume that real estate will constantly appreciate and never go down, or that if they don't buy "now" the opportunity will never arise again. History shows that real estate markets fluctuate over time. Waiting for the market to slow and correct itself, so real estate can be purchased at more favorable prices, can pay substantial dividends.

Keep in mind that house affordability, along with the price of the property, is determined by the income of the mortgage borrower and the prevailing interest rates of the mortgage when it is first taken out and again when it comes due for renewal.

Getting caught with higher interest rates just as their mortgage comes due is one of the most common causes of concern for average homeowners.

A consumer who originally took a term mortgage of five years when the interest rate was low may experience serious problems if the interest rate rises by the time the mortgage becomes due for renewal. For example, based on a household income that qualified you for a $300,000 mortgage at a 5 percent yearly interest rate when the mortgage loan was originally taken, prospective owners can qualify for a mortgage of only about $255,000 if the interest rate rises to 6 percent at renewal time. If the interest rate rises to 7 percent, they could qualify for only about $240,000.

If homeowners are unable to pay the difference between the original mortgage of $300,000 and the one they can qualify for at renewal time, they must make up for the difference by an alternative (high-ratio) mortgage loan. Otherwise, the bank could call the mortgage off by placing the real estate for sale as if owners had defaulted.

Government-guaranteed high-ratio loans are usually the last resort for those facing considerable shortfalls come mortgage renewal time, but obtaining this type of loan has its challenges. The mortgage applicant must prove sufficient income to carry monthly obligations and have a good credit rating; furthermore, the mortgage required must not exceed 85 percent or, in some rare cases, 95 percent of the appraised value of the property.

Before buying, prospective homeowners should first consider their job security and budget their income carefully. Again, allocating 33 percent of a pre-tax household income toward the carrying costs of the real estate property is the best way to make a safe purchase. Buyers are strongly advised not to fall for "no down payment" pitches. Such inflated purchases, almost as a rule, cause people to go beyond the affordability index of 33 percent, putting themselves in the precarious position of compromising their quality of life to meet the carrying cost of unaffordable, high-priced real estate purchases.

No-down-payment schemes are designed by desperate or greedy sellers who have no other way to sell their real estate products at high prices. They lure people with little or no money into real estate ownership, which can be abruptly terminated by even the slightest economic change.

Buyers who cannot provide a down payment of at least 25 percent of the purchase price, or whose income is not sufficient to carry financing according to a reasonable affordability index, are advised to wait, even if it takes years to accumulate enough savings to purchase their homes. This will help ensure that, one day, they will be able to protect themselves and their families behind a shield of down-payment equity along with sufficient wages and job security.

The above is particularly applicable to buyers with children, who under no circumstances should jeopardize their family's safety net. Financial hardship, including the possibility of losing the roof above their heads, can lead to unpleasant, even traumatic experiences for children and spouses.

It is a different story for buyers who are single or couples with no children who are absolutely determined to attain as much equity as possible in their home by using all available resources to pay down their mortgage as quickly as possible. They may do so conscientiously, knowing that their temporary hardship will yield fruit one day by freeing or substantially reducing their liability under the mortgage. Such examples are to be saluted, as long as these buyers remain aware of their financial capability and limitations.

For example, slaving to pay off or reduce your mortgage over an extended period may have a lasting effect on your quality of life. Is it worth it to sacrifice all available resources and deprive yourself of your basic necessities as well as clothing, education, traveling, vacations, and entertainment? It may be, especially when said buyers are younger and without children, and provided that the sacrifices continue after the arrival of children.

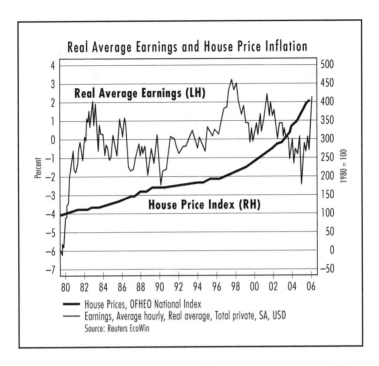

Real Average Earnings and House Price Inflation

Real Average Earnings (LH)

House Price Index (RH)

■ House Prices, OFHEO National Index
— Earnings, Average hourly, Real average, Total private, SA, USD
Source: Reuters EcoWin

The chart above indicates that average earnings have grown very slowly since 1983. In fact, in some instances, real wages have actually declined. Meanwhile, by the beginning of 2006, house prices had risen dramatically. Under normal conditions, the slow growth of income would not allow rapid expansion of consumer spending in real estate – unless it is founded entirely on cheap credit.

Generally, housing affordability begins to deteriorate as price increases outstrip gains in household income and the cost of long-term mortgages rises.[9]

At the beginning of the 1980s, the personal saving rates of consumers in the U.S. were at an all-time high; by the

---

9 Grant, 2007.

year 2005, they were at an all-time low. In fact, the average household saving ratio in the U.S. was actually negative. The main reason for such a turnaround in household saving is the fact that unprecedented inflation in housing prices has depleted U.S. households of their savings and housing in general has become less and less affordable. This chart is a chilling depiction of the erosion of affordability.

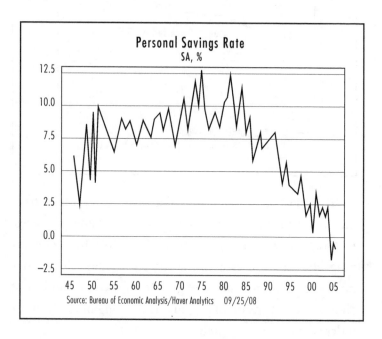

Consumers who are highly leveraged, especially by high-ratio mortgages, or interest-only mortgages at variable rates, will be seriously challenged in the future during cycles of market corrections.

The following graph measures the composite value of residential real estate in 20 urban areas in the U.S., showing the peak in sales in 2006 and 2007, and the decline since.

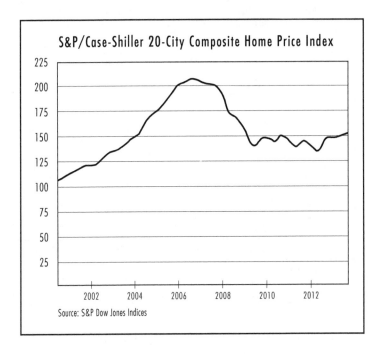

The table that follows – Income, Home Price, and Down Payment Guide – shows the maximum home price you can afford given a particular household income and based on down payments of either 10 percent or 25 percent. As previously discussed, I strongly warn against buying with 10 percent down or less, because of the risk associated with such small down payment equity, namely, the lack of a safety cushion should the economy turn bad or interest rates go up.

Income, Home Price, and Down Payment Guide				
Household Income	10% Down Payment	Maximum Home Price	25% Down Payment	Maximum Home Price
$25,000	$6,300	$63,000	$18,900	$75,600
$30,000	$8,200	$82,000	$24,700	$98,800
$35,000	$10,100	$101,000	$30,300	$121,200
$40,000	$12,000	$120,000	$36,000	$144,000
$45,000	$13,900	$139,000	$41,700	$166,800
$50,000	$15,800	$158,000	$47,400	$189,600
$60,000	$19,600	$196,000	$58,800	$235,200
$70,000	$23,400	$234,000	$70,100	$280,400
$80,000	$27,200	$272,000	$81,500	$326,000
$90,000	$31,000	$310,000	$92,800	$371,200
$100,000	$34,800	$348,000	$104,300	$417,200

Figures are rounded to the nearest $100.
All figures are based on a mortgage interest rate of 8 percent amortized 25 years and the mortgage a buyer would qualify for based on a 32 percent debt to service ratio.

The example is given for mortgages taken at an 8 percent interest rate, which is a fair measure of safety notwithstanding that prevailing mortgage rates may be much lower. For all practical purposes, if you factor in the original real estate closing costs, which run in the thousands, the effective interest rate to the buyers becomes higher. Today's low interest rates are a desperate move on the part of the government to keep the economy afloat and are not going to last forever.

Closing costs may include the mortgage arranging fees, insurance, home inspection fees, legal costs and disbursements, property transfer tax, land transfer tax, life insurance, and property and fire insurance. Those closing costs can range anywhere from 1.5 to 3.5 percent of the total cost of your property.

Factoring in the above out-of-pocket closing costs for the first year, and anticipating the future rise in mortgage interest rates, it is only prudent to be cautious and assume that residential mortgages may reach 8 percent, perhaps more, in times to come. During close to 40 years of being involved in real estate and observing its trends, I have witnessed fluctuating mortgage interest rates for substantial periods of time.

Again, the main reason that mortgage interest rates have been so low for the past decade or so is that governments are desperate to safeguard the economy from total collapse.

In the last ten years or so, the price of real estate, mostly due to rampant speculation, has risen dramatically. The only way to maintain such overpriced, expensive homes and make them look affordable is to have them financed at very low interest rates. Eventually, the real estate market will go through price corrections and recover, but for owners who are not locked into low interest rates for an extended period, inflationary trends during the rise of interest rates will present a very real problem.

I have been observing real estate trends for over four decades and have witnessed interest rates on first mortgages fluctuate anywhere from 3 percent to 18 percent. In fact, there were long periods when they lingered in the 8 to 10 percent range. It is for this very reason that the above chart was chosen and based on an 8 percent interest rate.

If you look closely at your household income, taking into

consideration 10 and 25 percent down payments, the chart will show you the maximum home price that you can afford. Moreover, you will find that the suggested maximum home prices are by far lower than the prices currently prevalent in major urban areas. Consumers should concentrate on prices suggested in the above chart, even if that means waiting for market corrections to occur in order for prices to come down.

You should remember that it is only a question of time before the interest rates will go up. Owning expensive real estate with high interest rate mortgages will spell serious hardship for the many people who get caught in such a position.

The Overall Cost of a Mortgage Loan

Many first-time real estate buyers can afford small down payments only. To facilitate purchases, buyers turn to financial institutions for high-ratio, more expensive mortgages. In addition, they pay default insurance premiums on such mortgages. These small down payments leave a huge 95 to 100 percent debt on the property. Paying that debt off – or, in other words, amortizing such mortgage loans – requires an extended period, typically 25 years and sometimes even up to 35 years, depending on the mortgage contract with the mortgage lender.

It is important to note that the longer the term of the mortgage, the more expensive the mortgage loan becomes. To make monthly payments more affordable, many financial institutions have allowed longer-term mortgage repayment plans, some even up to 40 years. Think about it. If you take such a long-term mortgage loan out at age 30, you'd be pretty long in the tooth by the time you paid it off, unless somewhere down the line you accelerated your payments or sold the property in the hopes of making a profit.

By allowing homeowners to make lower monthly payments over longer periods, financial institutions have greatly indebted them. Long-term mortgages translate into a considerable increase in the overall interest paid on the mortgages in comparison with unit owners who were able to afford higher monthly payments by taking their mortgages at shorter terms, such as 15 or 20 years.

Mortgage payments are usually payable on a monthly basis, and, most commonly, they include the portion of the principal and monthly increment of yearly interest. The actual debt is reduced only as the amount of principal is paid off. Over time, this reduction builds equity in the property. During the first six or seven years of payments, most of the money contributed goes toward paying interest. Starting at about seven years, the payout of the principal starts to increase substantially every year and thereby accelerates the payout of the overall debt. Eventually, by reducing the mortgage debt, the equity in the property becomes larger. By the time owners finish paying the mortgage, they likely will have paid four or six times the original amount borrowed, depending on the interest rates and amortization schedules.

Mortgage loans with interest-only payments will always stand still at their original face value. There will be no appreciation of equity unless such equity is created by favorable market conditions driving the value of real estate prices higher.

Note that the words "term," "due date," and "amortization period" should not be confused. The "amortization period" is the time in years over which the principal and interest payments are calculated – usually not less than 15 years and not more than 30 years. The longer the amortization period, the greater the overall interest cost of the borrowed money. "Term" is the period during which the conditions of the actual mortgage agreement legally bind the lender and the borrower. This usually ranges from two to five years.

The "due date" is the last day of the term, on which date the whole outstanding principal balance becomes due and payable unless the terms of the mortgage are extended by a further agreement in writing between the lender and the borrower. As of the due date, the lender has the option of leaving everything the same for a new term; not renewing the mortgage agreement and requiring the borrower to go elsewhere to pay off the outstanding principal by the due date; or offering the borrower better terms and conditions to renew with the same lender for a further term. As of the due date, the borrower has the option of remaining with the same lender or moving to a new one.

CHAPTER 4

Owning a Condo
vs. Renting an Apartment

Investing vs. Renting: "In Principal"

For many people, it is more advantageous to own rather than rent property. Over time, the value of property appreciates, and equity in the property increases as monthly mortgage payments gradually reduce the principal amount of the mortgage. Renters, in contrast, pay a set monthly amount to the owner for use of the space. Instead of building their own equity in the rented property, they are helping the apartment building owner build equity.

But on the other side of the coin, the renter remains worry free with regard to mortgage payments, maintenance costs, taxes, assessments, and fluctuating interest rates. The privilege of peacefully enjoying the rented premises at a set monthly rate may be more advantageous to some than tying themselves to often considerable and unpredictable financial obligations.

It all comes down to a matter of principal and afford-ability. While most people buy property to build equity or wealth, others choose to build their wealth by saving or investing in business opportunities other than real estate.

To those who think that, over time, real estate is a better asset than the stock market, consider this: $100,000 invested in Coca-Cola stock in 1990 was worth $1 million by the year 2000. Of course, it would have taken one hell of a fortune-teller to convince an investor to put that kind of money into the stock market and all on one stock, to begin with.

This is perhaps an extreme example, and I am by no means suggesting that investing in the stock market is always better than real estate. The fact of the matter is that any investment carries risk.

This chapter tells the story of Mr. Jones and Mr. Smith as a case study of renting vs. owning.

Mr. Jones owns a condominium unit. Mr. Smith rents a unit of the same size in the same complex. The following comparison is based on a five-year period and may apply equally to individuals with small or no equity and those with larger equity in their condominium units. In our example, both Mr. Jones and Mr. Smith start with $67,000 in their savings accounts and earn similar wages, which makes them financially equal.

Mr. Jones decides to invest his savings in the purchase of a condominium unit.

Mr. Smith decides to invest his savings in municipal bonds and use the investment and the interest they earn to defray his rental obligation. The municipal bonds yield 5 percent per year and mature in five years. For the sake of this case study, even though his monetary return is realized at the end of a five-year period, we will consider it to count as recouping his rent paid during that period.

Mr. Jones buys his condominium unit for $250,000 with a 25 percent down payment equaling $62,500. In addition, he incurs the closing costs, such as legal fees, mortgage arranging fees, land transfer tax, and other disbursements, all totaling about $4,500. Therefore, his total out-of-pocket cash investment is $67,000, the actual amount of money he had in his savings account before the purchase.

He obtains a five-year term mortgage for the balance of the purchase price of $187,500, amortized over 25 years at a 5.5 percent yearly interest rate with a monthly payment of $1,132, including principal and interest combined.[10] In addition, Mr. Jones is responsible for a $350 monthly maintenance fee, plus realty taxes of $150 per month. His total monthly obligation comes to $1,632.

After five years (60 months), his carrying cost amounts to $97,920. If we add to that his down payment and closing cost of $67,000, Mr. Jones' overall financial exposure amounts to $164,920.

In comparison, by paying a fixed monthly rent of $1,400, Mr. Smith spends $84,000 during those same five years (60 months) on his rental accommodation cost. Having invested his available cash of $67,000 into municipal bonds, his overall financial exposure after five years amounts to $151,000.

---

10 The term "interest rate and amortization schedule" was selected by the author for illustrative purposes. The mortgage repayment calculations are taken from the tables published by the Financial Publishing Company, a division of Carleton Inc.

The difference in financial exposure between them over five years comes to $13,920, in favor of Mr. Smith. This difference is important to remember, because, notwithstanding Mr. Jones's equity position after five years, his overall financial exposure was higher. From this perspective, Mr. Smith comes out ahead of Mr. Jones.

Let's look more closely at Mr. Jones, assuming favorable, and then unfavorable market conditions.

The Effects on Mr. Jones of Favorable Market Conditions

Let's assume that, for the first five years, there are no adverse changes in Mr. Jones's condominium complex – in other words, no special assessments are levied against his unit – and his maintenance fees, mortgage interest rates, and realty taxes remain steady and unchanged. Let's also assume favorable market conditions during those years – that property values appreciate according to traditional trends.

After the first five years, by making regular mortgage payments, Mr. Jones's principal on the mortgage is reduced by $20,250. The principal amount remaining on his mortgage after five years therefore drops to $167,250. His original down payment of $62,500 and the paid-off principal of $20,250 now represent the paid equity that he has in his condominium unit, namely, $82,750.

We could add to that a traditional 2 percent increase in real estate appreciation per year, which in five years amounts to 10 percent, or $25,000, so the value of Mr. Jones's condominium unit after five years increases to $275,000, in which he owns a total apparent equity of $107,750, or close to 39 percent.

Under these favorable market conditions, the difference in Mr. Jones's overall financial exposure ($13,920), in comparison with Mr. Smith, has been fully recouped. So is his closing cost of $4,500 to buy the unit.

If he sells his unit after five years, Mr. Jones will make a profit of $25,000, representing the difference between the original price of $250,000 and the unit's increased value of $275,000, putting him way ahead of Mr. Smith, who, as we will see, is barely able to cover his total five-year accommodation from his investment.

In fact, at the end of the first five-year period, Mr. Jones's equity might have appreciated even more if he had taken the mortgage at the lower, variable interest rate, or the market value of his unit had appreciated at a higher rate due to exceptionally high demand.

During the following five-year period, projections look even better for Mr. Jones because the original down payment and closing costs are not "repeat expenditures." His overall financial exposure will be lowered to $97,920, representing the carrying cost of looking after mortgage payments, maintenance fees, and real estate taxes.

If market conditions remain favorable, he'll accumulate greater equity due to the accelerated progression of the payments on the principal of the mortgage and the traditional market appreciation of his unit.

The Effects on Mr. Jones of
Unfavorable Market Conditions

However, in the event of adverse market conditions, the value of Mr. Jones's condominium unit may depreciate. Real estate is a volatile industry. Market corrections, such as occasional booms and busts, can be expected, though it is hard to predict when they will occur and how long they will last.

Instead of the traditional market appreciation during the first five years of Mr. Jones's condominium ownership, the market might experience a slowdown and subsequent correction.

In cases like this, properties lose value, sometimes quite rapidly. The loss of value may be quite severe, as witnessed in many urban areas of the U.S. from 2006 onward, when property value, especially of condominiums, decreased as much as 50 percent.

If Mr. Jones finds himself in such an adverse situation, he may lose the amount of his down payment. Furthermore, he will not gain from the traditional market equity buildup. In fact, his incurred losses may run into thousands of dollars.

It is fair to state that Mr. Jones's financial well being in preserving and maintaining the value of his condominium unit depends on quite a few variables: the state of the economy, market trends, mortgage interest rates, his job security, and the quality of the management and governance of his condominium complex together with the timing and duration of his ownership in relation to market trends.

If the market depreciates 15 percent in the five years after Mr. Jones buys his condominium unit, the unit will be worth

$37,500 less, due to depreciation, or $212,500. Therefore his apparent equity cannot possibly be more than $212,500 less the outstanding mortgage principal of 167,250, or $42,250. And this despite the fact that he made a $67,000 down payment and paid off a further $20,250 of the mortgage principal.

At that level of depreciation, Mr. Jones's starting investment of $67,000, plus $20,250 he paid over five years to reduce the principal of his mortgage, erodes considerably from its total of $87,250, leaving him with $45,250 in reduced equity after five years.

In comparison, Mr. Smith's original cash investment appreciates exactly the same as it would have during favorable market conditions. Although his cash investment and its appreciation on his overall rental accommodation cost are fully utilized and exhausted after five years, he lived in and enjoyed the rented unit of equal value and paid $13,920 less for his overall accommodation over five years.

The Effects on Mr. Smith of Unfavorable Market Conditions

An interesting situation could develop for Mr. Smith should the real estate market and economy turn for the worse. This would create more vacant condominium units, giving Mr. Smith a chance to rent the very same condominium for a lower price, perhaps $1,200 per month. Inflationary trends may drive interest rates up, giving his investments a higher yield. In this scenario, he likely ends up with a sizeable surplus after five years, rather than a very small shortfall. The market conditions that could affect Mr. Jones adversely, as an owner, may work to the benefit of Mr. Smith, as a renter.

Who Fares Better After Five Years?

It is all about timing. If markets experience exceptionally favorable appreciation due to high demand and low interest rates, Mr. Jones ends up much better off than Mr. Smith. Overall prices may have gone up by as much as 30 percent, as they did from 2000 to 2006.

Financial Breakdown During Favorable Market Conditions			
Mr. Jones		**Mr. Smith**	
Condominium purchase price	$250,000	Rents equally valued unit	$250,000
25% down payment	$62,500	Commits to invest his savings in municipal bonds	$67,000
Closing costs	$4,500		
Initial investment	$67,000	Initial investment	$67,000
Carrying Cost			
Monthly blended payment on $187,500 mortgage at 5.5% yearly interest rate	$1,132		
Monthly maintenance fee	$350		
Monthly real estate taxes	$150	Monthly rental payment	$1,400
Total monthly payment	$1,632	Total monthly payment	$1,400
Carrying cost over 5 years	$97,920	Accommodation cost over 5 years	$84,000
Overall Financial Exposure over 5 Years			
Initial investment ($67,000) plus 5-year carrying cost ($97,920)	$164,920	Accommodation cost ($84,000) plus investment in bonds ($67,000)	$151,000
Enhancement of Equity		**Earnings from Investment**	
Paydown on mortgage principal (5 years)	$20,250	Yield on $67,000 investment in municipal bonds at 5% interest	$16,750
Market Appreciation 2% over (5 years)	$25,000	Recouped original cash invested	$67,000
Total enhancement	$45,250	Total earnings after 5 years	$83,750
Condo value after 5 years (original purchase price plus market appreciation)	$275,000	Total accommodation cost over 5 years	$84,000
Profit, if sold after 5 years	$25,000	Shortfall after 5 years	$250
Total liability/Equity After 5 Years (60 Months)			
Remaining mortgage liability	$167,250	Liability	$0
Apparent equity in condominium unit	$107,750	Cash remaining from the original $67,000 investment	$0

But what if they had moved into their units in 1988? During the following five years, Mr. Jones likely would have lost about 30 percent of the value of his unit due to depreciation caused by adverse market conditions. This would have wiped out his equity. The same can be said for the five-year period, starting in 2006, when real estate catastrophically lost as much as 50 percent of its value in many U.S. cities.

Financial Breakdown During Unfavorable Market Conditions			
Mr. Jones		Mr. Smith	
Condominium purchase price	$250,000	Rents equally valued unit	$250,000
25% down payment	$62,500	Commits to invest his savings in municipal bonds	$67,000
Closing costs	$4,500		
Initial investment	$67,000	Initial accommodation cost	$67,000
Carrying Cost			
Monthly blended payment on $187,500 mortgage at 5.5% yearly interest rate	$1,132		
Monthly maintenance fee	$350		
Monthly real estate taxes	$150	Monthly rental payment	$1,400
Total monthly payments	$1,632	Total monthly payment	$1,400
Carrying cost over 5 years	$97,920	Accommodation cost over 5 years	$84,000
Overall Financial Exposure over 5 Years			
Initial ($67,000) investment plus 5 year carrying cost ($97,920)	$164,920	Accommodation cost ($84,000) plus invested bonds (($67,000)	$151,000
Erosion of Equity		Earnings from Investment	
Original condo value	$250,000	Yield on $67,000 investment in municipal bonds at 5% interest	$16,750
Market depreciation 15% over 5 years	$37,500	Recouped original cash invested	$67,000
Condo value after depreciation	$212,500	Total cash return in 5 years	$83,750
Initial investment ($67,000) plus pay down of mortgage principal over 5 year ($20,250)	$87,250		
15% market depreciation	$37,500	Total accommodation cost over 5 yrs	$84,000
Monetary loss if sold after 5 years	$49,750	Shortfall after 5 years	$250
Total Liability/Equity After 5 Years (60 Months)			
Remaining mortgage liability	$167,250	Liability	$0
Apparent equity in condominium unit	$42,250	Cash remaining from the original $67,000 investment	$0

As you can see in the above example, equity, in the short run, is not always based purely on paying off the principal of the mortgage. Equity is directly dependent on the property's value, which is largely affected by prevailing market conditions. Buying into real estate for the short-term purpose of building equity is essentially gambling on the state of the economy, interest rates, and market conditions.

On May 11, 2011, the Web edition of the *New York Times* posted a very interesting analysis of buying vs. renting. According to the paper's calculator, renting seems to be more advantageous for people who do not plan to stay in the same premises for more than four to five years, and buying is more advantageous for those who decide to stay for a longer period.[11]

Investing vs. Renting: The Long-term Truth

Real estate market trends are influenced, not only by unemployment and interest rates, but also by demand, the cost of building materials and supplies, inflationary trends, and many other factors. These are complex market relationships. Even the best financial analysts do not have the precise answers when it comes to predicting market trends.

Things definitely tilt in a property owner's favor over a longer period, regardless of the economy and periodical market swings. Owners of real estate properties gradually build up the benefit of equity as the principal of the mortgage debt is reduced and eventually paid off over time.

After about seven years, payments on the principal

---

11 Quealy & Tse, 2011.

reduction of the mortgage become more prominent and, depending on the amortization period of the mortgage, the principal henceforth will be reduced more rapidly. Depending on the amortization period, if the buyer hangs on for 15, 20, 25, or even 35 years, they will have accomplished the goal of living in their property while simultaneously lowering their mortgage debt and eventually paying it off.

Historically, real estate has appreciated in the range of 1.5 to 4 percent per year except for periodic market corrections. Consumer wages were supposed to follow, but, unfortunately, this has not quite happened. Are consumer wages going to increase in the future to keep pace with overall inflationary real estate trends? Historically speaking, you should not be optimistic.

In the meantime, buyers should exercise common sense when buying property, whether for investment purposes or for personal accommodation. They must be in tune with the marketplace and the state of the economy. The most opportune and favorable time to buy is during a so-called buyer's market, when many real estate products, including condominiums, are offered at cheaper prices. Buying when the market is high and "going with the flow," hoping that prices will continue to rise, may not be such a good idea. You cannot predict to a fine degree of certainty when the market will level off and possibly take a downward turn.

Oversupply is one of the most important factors you should watch for when buying any real estate product. An oversupplied market is a buyer's market. An undersupplied market is a seller's market.

In our example of Mr. Jones and Mr. Smith, Mr. Smith did not lose any sleep worrying about mortgage interest rates or market conditions. If he elects to rent again, he presumably will save another $67,000 over five years as he patiently awaits the arrival of a buyer's market to buy his own unit or remains in his rental unit, taking comfort in knowing that his future rental is pre-set and worry free.

As said before, the comparison of Mr. Jones and Mr. Smith applies equally to individuals buying condominium units with little or no down payment and those who purchase their units with a sizeable down payment. The only difference is that the former may lose their units and accumulate great financial liability if the market turns on them, whereas the latter may lose some or even all of their invested and earned equity but are in a better position to remain in their unit and weather the storm.

It is important to note that it is not disadvantageous to rent rather than buy, especially during times of inflated and unaffordable real estate prices. Determining whether to invest or rent in relation to condominium living should be a personal decision based on a clear understanding of the factors, quality information, and a clear perception of one's values at the time of the intended purchase.

By learning about the cost of maintenance fees, realty taxes, prevailing interest rates, and the conditions of the market, you should be able to draw a reasonably sound conclusion about whether to buy or rent.

Apartment Buildings vs. Condo Buildings

Last, but not least, it is useful to compare apartment buildings and condo buildings.

Owners of apartment buildings are usually business-savvy real estate professionals. Whether private person(s) or corporate entities, in most cases they have owned and operated apartment buildings for years. Many corporate apartment owners relegate the day-to-day care of their buildings to an inside or outside management team. They carefully monitor the management team's performance to ensure that expenses related to maintenance and repairs are within projected budgets.

The owner can simply terminate the management team's contract if the team does not perform in an honest, responsible, and professional fashion.

Properly run apartment buildings seldom exceed yearly expenses in excess of 55 percent of the yearly income received from the tenants. These expenses include costs for necessary maintenance, repairs, periodical replacements, the superintendent's salary, management fees, professional fees (such as legal and accounting), and the payment of real estate taxes.

What about major repairs that the reserve budget cannot meet? Apartment building owners may take out a mortgage loan, possibly in addition to existing financing, to cover these expenses. Or, if they are strapped financially or are unwilling to cover the expenses, they can sell the building in whatever state of repair it is in. In contrast to condominiums, the owners of apartment buildings can decide the fate of their building themselves.

Traditionally, the average markup on the sale of an apartment building has been about $5,000 to $20,000 per apartment unit. But what if the apartment building were improved and converted into a condominium? Each condo unit could be sold for hundreds of thousands of dollars more. This is why many apartment building owners decide to convert their buildings into condominiums. They often can qualify for a permit to make this conversion by performing very slight improvements. Unfortunately, such massive conversions are a major cause for the depletion of available affordable rental apartment units.

Who wins? The owners who convert their building into a condo. They are now worry-free concerning the maintenance of the building. These responsibilities have been shifted onto the shoulders of the unit buyers, who also become the owners of the whole property, including the land and the building, commonly referred to as a condominium complex.

CHAPTER 5

How Long Will Condos Last?

Condominiums will exist as an ownership option as long as there are buyers who are willing to buy them and accept their ownership-related perils. Condominium ownership, in its present form, will be viable as long as monthly maintenance fees and realty taxes remain below the monthly rental of a comparable unit in a condominium complex or apartment building. If maintenance costs exceed the cost of comparative rentals, most of the condominium units are likely to be rented out. Buying into such condominium complexes is financially risky: the very notion of "condominium ownership" becomes purely academic once the demand to purchase them no longer exists.

As far as physical longevity goes, all buildings have a finite lifespan. Condominium owners must understand that, as a result of wear and tear, their complex will not be the same forever. This doesn't necessarily mean that, eventually, the entire complex will be brought down by a demolition company's sledgehammers. However, by the time a condominium complex is 40 years old, it will have gone through several partial or complete retrofits, likely in stages.

Bearing posts, outside walls, and floors may remain structurally sound for many years, but the elevators, roof, balconies, façade, windows, mechanical components, and other interior elements will need to be refurbished or replaced from time to time. In that sense, the very economics of maintaining a condominium unit dictates the viability of its usefulness and affordability. It is not uncommon for condo unit owners in such expensive-to-maintain complexes to sell their unit and rent a less expensive apartment unit. In older complexes, the question may arise whether it would be more economical to demolish the whole structure and rebuild it from scratch. Individual unit owners are likely to be divided on the issue. They may be unwilling or unable to pay the cost of such a major undertaking. Eventually, these owners may be given a simple choice: sell your unit at whatever price is offered or face the consequences of default. This is a perfect example of an unfriendly takeover in the making.

Individual condo unit owners cannot avail themselves of the traditional homeowner's ability, in times of financial hardship, to neglect the maintenance of their property without the risk of losing it. Condo owners are obligated to contribute to common maintenance and upkeep every month.

There will always be unit owners with deeper pockets,

able to afford higher maintenance costs and special assessments. Likewise, there will always be unit owners who are strapped for cash and therefore in peril of losing their unit.

Condominium ownership can remain viable as long as the majority of the unit owners in a complex can weather periodic economic storms. Major real estate crashes, such as those of the 1930s and early 1990s – as well as the most recent American crash, which started in 2006 – do not repeat themselves often. However, no one can say with certainty that another one may not be around the corner.

Condominium owners, therefore, should always be prepared for future adverse market conditions that may severely test their financial strength.

Winding Down: Termination

Eventually, over a period of decades, the escalating costs of repairs and maintenance of the aged complex may become so great that owners will not be able to afford it. Ideally, the condominium corporation will realize ahead of time that the complex is deteriorating and that it is no longer viable to maintain the structure and its common elements. The majority of the unit owners may then agree that their condominium entity should be terminated and the remaining assets, most significantly the land on which the complex is situated, be sold for the benefit of all the owners. The proceeds from the sale would then be divided among them on a pro-rated basis.

Some complexes can experience deterioration much sooner than expected, particularly if they were not properly built and properly maintained. Structural damages due to roof leaks and inadequate insulation may make the complexes unfit for human habitation. Even the best-constructed and managed complexes will eventually see their end as common elements and mechanical structures become unsafe and prohibitively expensive to fix.

The outcome of a given winding-down scenario will depend on whether the remaining individual unit owners have the financial strength and business sense to carry on. Otherwise, they will need to terminate their obsolete complex by liquidating its assets.

Adverse Market Conditions: A 100-Unit Example

Besides physical deterioration due to wear and tear, consider what may happen to an average 100-unit condominium complex during extended adverse market conditions. The year is 1989, and the condominium complex is fairly new. For the sake of simplicity, let us say that each condominium unit is purchased for $300,000. Within a few months, the local market becomes saturated with condominiums, and there are few or no buyers willing to buy units on the market.

Let us say that 50 unit owners bought their units with more than a 25 percent down payment (call them Solid Equity Owners), 25 unit owners bought with a 25 percent down payment (call them Medium Equity Owners), and 25 unit owners bought with a small or no down payment (call them No Equity Owners).

Suppose that half of the unit owners have mortgages with short maturity dates and variable interest rates, whereas the other half have their mortgages at longer terms of fixed interest rates.

Note that many property owners take advantage of short-term, variable interest rate mortgages because they offer lower interest rates in comparison with long-term mortgages locked up at fixed interest rates. In real life, the interest rates of the majority of such variable mortgages are, from time to time, adjusted by the institution that provides them. When the prime bank's interest rates change, so do the rates on these mortgages.

Though they are cheaper because of their low interest rates, these mortgages pose a risk to real estate owners in the case of a sudden upward shift of interest rates. On the other hand, long-term mortgages at a fixed interest rate that mature in 5, 10, or even 15 years, although more expensive during periods of low prime rates, provide safety from unpredictable interest rate changes over time.

Variable Interest Rate Mortgages

First, consider the owners with variable interest rate mortgages. There is a sudden upward shift in interest rates. Some No Equity Owners, due to their inability to pay higher monthly mortgage payments, fall victim to financial hardship. Unable to service their expensive mortgage, they default on their monthly obligations.

In our example, these unit owners are the first to go, relinquishing their ownership by simply walking out or being expelled by power of sale or foreclosure procedures. In most cases, legal costs, real estate commissions, arrears on taxes, and arrears on maintenance fees claim whatever remaining value might be left in their unit upon the forced sale of the units by mortgage holders.

Suppose next that, due to an increase in interest rates, some of the Medium Equity Owners with variable interest mortgages also find it difficult to keep up with their monthly mortgage payments. Even though they originally put 25 percent cash down, ironically, they may find themselves in a worse position than those who put little or no money down. The market has gone into a slump and, due to a glut of available defaulted units, the overall value of units declines by the year 1991, wiping out their original 25 percent equity down payment. For those who chose short-term mortgages, their depressed equity payment no longer represents (sufficient) equity to obtain mortgages at fixed rates and a longer term when their mortgage comes up for renewal.

Small equity in volatile markets may be insufficient security for even the biggest risk-taking mortgage lenders. The only way out for these unfortunate owners, short of losing their units, is to apply for a high-ratio (usually 90 to 95 percent of the value) government-insured mortgage loan, provided that their jobs and the newly adjusted overall value of the units qualify them to do so. The high-ratio mortgage then pays off and replaces the existing mortgage on their units. As the original equity is lost due to adverse market conditions, previously Medium Equity Owners now become No Equity Owners.

Fixed Interest Rate Mortgages

Fast forward now to 1993, when the real estate market was seriously depressed. Our condominium complex suffers a multitude of financial hardships. The other 50 percent of the owners with the longer-term, fixed interest rate mortgages, provided that they held their jobs and were financially sound, may have been able to cope with the situation. Even though their units lost their equity or (resale) value due to market conditions, they can still afford to take a sit-and-wait attitude, solely protected by their longer-term mortgage and their individual financial strength.

Generally speaking, when more than 10 percent of the unit owners become insolvent, unable to carry monthly mortgage payments, and their mortgage holders sell such units at fire sale prices, the overall value of all the units in the complex diminishes. The market becomes risky, littered with multiple listings of such defaulted units. Buyers lose confidence in this kind of deflated market. The same unit that was purchased in the complex for $300,000 in 1989 may be worth only $200,000 by 1994, losing as much as one-third of its original value.

A particularly challenging problem arises for unit owners with a fixed interest rate mortgage by 1994, when most of the usual five-year term fixed interest rate mortgages come due for renewal. Even though the interest rates may remain favorable, the overall receding value of the units causes banks to consider existing mortgages too high and, therefore, too risky to renew. Most will likely commit to renewals of mortgages by no more than 75 percent of the current market value based on the prevailing market values.

As a result, the unit owners with less than one-third equity in their units are faced with a serious financial problem of covering for the shortfall – the difference between the original mortgage and their now heavily discounted renewal mortgage.

Practically speaking, from the original value of $300,000 in 1989, the units may have lost up to one-third of their value by 1994, at the end of the five-year term, when most mortgages come up for renewal or refinancing. Many units will then be worth only $200,000 at renewal time. As most mortgage lenders will renew the existing mortgages at only 75 percent of the value or, in our case, $150,000, the unit owner will be required to pay, out of pocket, the difference needed to cover for the shortfall between their originally advanced mortgage and the adjusted renewal mortgage of $150,000. Otherwise, the mortgage company will not renew.

In the absence of available cash, the unit owner will be forced to scramble for a personal loan or a more expensive second mortgage, if it can be obtained at all.

Most of the No Equity Owners, with existing high-ratio mortgages, will face losing their property outright, unable to bail themselves out. The Medium Equity Owners, who put down payments of 25 percent or more, will be forced to take out more expensive high-ratio mortgages. Otherwise, due to the shortage of available cash to cover for the shortfall between the original and new mortgage, they will be subject to foreclosure procedures. Our sample complex, originally consisting of 50 percent of Solid and Medium Equity Owners, by 1994 eventually comprises mainly No Equity Owners with high-ratio mortgages.

The original No Equity Owners who lost their units face an even grimmer reality. Their accumulated debts, due to defaults on maintenance fees and mortgage payments, will be so large that most of them, after being foreclosed, evicted, and sued, will be personally liable for the deficit between their overall debt and the fire-sale price of their former unit. Personal liability may run in the thousands of dollars. Many of these hapless former unit owners will be haunted for years by judgements and bad credit.

The unsold, vacant units in our sample complex eventually become rock-bottom bargains with many vacancies or rented units, often bought by real estate speculators and ordinary buyers taking advantage of prices that are now in line with the affordable housing index.

Over the next several years, consumer confidence rises, the need for more units arises, and market conditions improve. Previously unwanted vacant units are eventually sold. To keep up with the new demand thus created, construction of new condominium units begins anew. Those who managed to survive in our sample complex may begin, from the year 2004 and onward, to slowly recoup their unit values and the original equity they put in them by way of down payments.

This example is not an academic exercise; it is a fair reflection of the major urban North American market climate from 1989 to 1995, when condominium units, on average, lost 20 to 35 percent in value, only to regain their original value over an extended period of time.

Our 100-unit example shows that unit owners who put

solid down payments on their units were not as seriously affected by the market decline as others who invested small or medium down payments and lost their units.

Most of the Solid Equity Owners could remortgage their units at the same amount as originally obtained because of the sufficient equity they originally put in their units. Medium Equity Owners, who did not have readily available cash to cover for the difference between the original mortgage and the lower, newly adjusted mortgage at the renewal date, would have had to scramble for money or remortgage their units with more expensive, high-ratio mortgages.

Many No Equity Owners would have to go through unpleasant, involuntary foreclosure procedures, losing not only their units but finding themselves liable for the deficits and shortfalls from the resulting sales of their former units.

Fluctuating Prices Over Time

Statistically speaking, the prices of real estate in general have been appreciating on average by 2 to 5 percent per year, depending on the location. During good economic times, appreciation can be even greater. There are periods, however, when areas – primarily congested urban ones – undergo price changes also known as "corrections" – the euphemism for price declines. The next chart, New One-Family Houses: Median Sales Price, showing price changes over time, shows how the market goes up and down. Each wave consists of a series of up-and-down movements in increments of a few months or so, keeping average real estate investors in suspense as to the value of their property.

A practical problem faced by both experts and non-experts is the inability to determine exactly when the market has reached the bottom and the recovery has begun. If you take a close look at the figure that follows, you will see that recoveries from slumps go into a seemingly continuous upward line; however, looking more closely, you will notice that the line oscillates, with frequent drops and lifts, in time spans ranging from just a few months to several years.

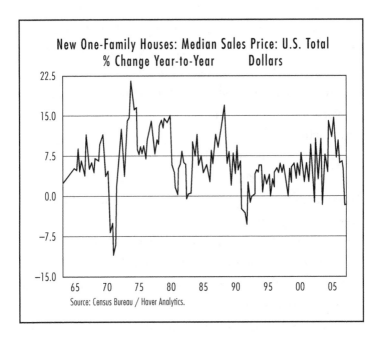

New One-Family Houses: Median Sales Price: U.S. Total
% Change Year-to-Year Dollars

Source: Census Bureau / Haver Analytics.

As may be seen in the figure, prices fluctuated upward to as much as 35 percent from 1970 to 1973, only to come down to 15 percent by 1975 and so forth, taking consumers on constant roller coaster rides. Average household income did not fluctuate so widely; in fact, it was either stagnant or moved modestly upward though not nearly enough to make homes affordable during periods of upward sale prices.

Affordability Factors Leading to Fluctuations

By 2006, housing affordability was more favorable compared with the 1980s. However, by fall 2006, the affordability index applicable to major urban areas had reached close to 50 percent. This is considered a trigger number that indicates the average household can no longer afford to buy and carry real estate without sacrificing quality of life and endangering their ability to provide food, clothing, education, and other necessities to their families.

You can blame the erosion of affordability on rising house prices, weakening household incomes, and higher borrowing costs.

Will the overall growth in the housing market regain its momentum and continue at the pace it experienced from 2000 to 2006? Most likely not. It is best to be cautious about the future, given the small but steady increases in interest rates, uncertain unemployment rates, and the potential of an oversupply of condominiums in the market.

Note that the historically low interest rates of the market over the past ten years or so are due mostly to desperate measures taken by the government to keep housing costs in check. Any substantial increase in interest rates would result in inflationary trends, leading to severe economic and market changes adversely affecting the housing sector and, thereby, the whole economy.

The Federal Reserve announced, on August 9, 2011, that,

to fend off such adversity, it would extend low rates up to 2013. According to noted economic analyst John Mauldin, this approach is "practically pushing people into high-risk assets in search for yield at precisely the time [the U.S.] may be slipping into another recession, which will put those assets at their highest risk."[12] The Fed's intention may present even higher problems to consumers, especially those who are close to retirement.

You cannot naively assume that pressures to keep interest rates low will last forever. Interest rates are not determined solely by the government. They are also influenced by international economic trends which are often unpredictable and volatile.

The next chart shows the fluctuating demand for U.S. sales of new homes from 1964 to 2006 as a percentage of GDP. You can see that, over the past 40 years, real estate slowdowns, often referred to as slumps, occurred in 1967, 1970, 1975, 1981, and 1982, and that the worst one before the 2006 American crash was in 1991.

---

12 In correspondence with the author dated August 20, 2011.

U.S. Sales of New Homes as a % of GDP

Source: Reuters EcoWin

By the end of 2006, the American market started to show another slump in the making. (Note the vertical drop of sales on the chart.) It turned out to be exceptionally severe. It was the catalyst that brought the whole U.S. economy to the brink of bankruptcy. As of early August 2011, Congress approved desperate measures, allowing trillions of dollars of new debt, to save the economy, while the housing slump continued to 2013, when it started to pick up again.

You can see that each slump was preceded by a period of strong sales and that slumps occurred quite frequently, often within a few months' time. The turnarounds may take many months, even years. In the case of the 1991 slump, it took 13 long years for the market to reach the previous highs of 1988.

Buying Frenzies Leading to Oversupply

During favorable economic times, especially with the real estate market on the upswing, condominium units can be bought with little or no down payment because of their substantial appreciation in value. To satisfy demand and keep abreast of other mortgage loaners, banks ease their lending criteria by approving little or no down payment purchases. This becomes a major contributing factor to uncontrolled speculative buying with small or no-equity participation.

Ordinary folk turn into speculative investors in droves, buying condominium units and other real estate hoping to ride a wave of success by selling them later at a higher price. In many instances, to attain a desired sale price over time, they take a calculated risk by renting out their newly acquired units, often for less than the total monthly carrying costs on the unit.

This is where the game of condominium speculation becomes dangerous. History shows that an oversupply of units may be created when over 30 percent of condominium units are bought by profit-hungry, small-time investors rushing to buy a product they don't need for themselves. Due to the sheer number of such investors-turned-speculators, the market enters an artificial state of (high) demand. At the first sign of an economic slowdown, these speculators retreat, bringing the buying frenzy to a halt. Suddenly, everybody realizes that there is actually no demand. In the resulting panic, investors dump their units onto the market, causing prices to plummet and wreaking havoc in the market. The glut of available units for sale is a signal to "legitimate" buyers that there is an oversupply of units.

Oversupply creates dangerous conditions in any economic sector, but especially in the real estate industry, which accounts for about 30 percent of the entire national economy. A condominium unit may be a commodity to an investor, but to most others, it's a home. High prices as a result of frenzied speculation mean that buyers wishing to live in their units must pay (artificially) inflated prices. When the economy slows down, carrying the payments on overpriced condominiums becomes a major issue, often detrimentally so for Small or No Equity Owners. As the market drops, small-time investors are the first to put their units up for sale. Others become worried about not being able to sell their units for the original purchase price. As a result, many of them put their units up for sale, hoping for the right buyer to come along.

Negative market turnarounds due to oversupply can happen very quickly, sometimes within a few months. An oversupplied or saturated market becomes a buyer's market with a multitude of choices. Naturally, buyers in such markets offer the lowest bids. Financially weak investors eventually succumb. Left with no other choice, they sell their units for lower prices, often at a loss.

Most speculative investors in this situation become panicky. In most cases, the rent they receive on their units cannot cover the mortgage payments and maintenance fees. Fearful that prices may drop to even lower levels, some are forced to sell at deficit prices, absorbing losses or liabilities to pay off existing mortgages; others are forced to put the units up for sale to prevent even greater personal liability down the road. A downtrend in the condominium market is established. The ensuing panic causes a loss of confidence in the market and, with many other frightened owners putting their units up for sale, the possibility of a market crash looms large.

Oversupply

Oversupply is one of the most dangerous conditions in the real estate market and generally a precursor to overall economic problems. Historically, many market slumps were caused by oversupply. When speculators buy too many units for the real market to absorb, it causes market saturation and, consequently, a sudden slowdown and even stoppage of construction. This often leads to (massive) layoffs and heavy losses to the construction and real estate sectors.

The real estate crash in the early 1990s is an example of a market collapse caused by oversupply. Condominiums were hugely affected. By the mid-1990s, some condominiums lost as much as 50 percent of their value compared with their worth in the late 1980s. In the wake of oversupply, severe consequential economic problems follow, an increase in the unemployment rate being the most notable. The most recent real estate crash in the U.S., which started in 2006, is an even better example.

Ironically, oversupply is often a by-product of a vibrant economy fueled by low interest rates. Low interest rates mean cheap credit, which lures ordinary people into becoming speculative investors in real estate commodities such as condominiums.

Cheap credit has its disadvantages, particularly when it is available for a long period and inspires speculative borrowing. During the borrowing phase, the economy seems to do fine. But sooner or later, the prices of things bought on credit reach (artificially) high levels. The ever-rising cost of building materials, labor, and land adds to the problem. The construction supply industry seizes the opportunity created by the real estate bonanza to raise its prices, which puts pressure on builders and developers to raise the prices of their real estate products.

Prices eventually stop rising when real estate products cease to be in demand – in other words, when they exceed the general housing affordability. The market then slows down, becomes stagnant, or crashes. Lenders and borrowers suffer losses. As the spending slows, it drags the economy down.

Real estate recoveries are built largely on cheap credit, which was the major reason the real estate market rebounded after the recession of the early 1990s. That's when the real estate bubble popped, causing the value of real estate products, particularly condominiums, to plummet dramatically. Ironically, the low interest rates that brought the economy out of the previous recession may be the cause of the next.

Oversupply of condominium units, aside from the greed of small-time speculative investors, may be caused by: the poorly planned progression of construction; depletion of natural demand by buyers wishing to become owner-residents, due to high market prices; and the government's failure to closely monitor the industry and curtail the ease with which consumers can obtain high-ratio financing.

Many would argue that, in a free market economy, governments should not regulate the market's supply and demand. However, high-ratio real estate loans, guaranteed by taxpayers' money, must be subject to government scrutiny because of the government's responsibility to taxpayers. If municipal governments can regulate the size and growth of residential subdivisions by putting restrictions on how many new housing startups can be built, then provincial and federal governments should be accountable for responsible economic policies when it comes to the taxpayer guaranties it provides to the banking sector. Nearly one-third of our economic well being depends directly on the housing industry; it is unacceptable, therefore, for governments to stand by during rampant, artificial growth in real estate in which speculative buyers haphazardly make risky purchases with little or no money down, de facto financing their mortgage debt with hard-earned taxpayer' monies.

Artificially created demand and, consequently, artificially inflated market prices, come exclusively at the expense of ordinary consumers who are looking for affordable condominium units and other forms of real estate. When prices rise too high, affordability is reduced and demand drops, slowing markets down.

Just how bad the affordability of housing can become is reflected in a *Wall Street Journal* article from June 2005, which reported that mortgage rates, at near record lows, were fueling prices and forcing families to stretch to buy homes. Regional studies performed in 2004 showed that mortgages in selected U.S. urban areas accounted for 99 percent of a home's value, up from 85 percent in 2001. That exactly "mirrored past conditions that preceded (previous) regional housing busts."

We now know what happened in the U.S. by 2007 – an enormous real estate crash. By 2013, it is still reverberating, and we may not see the end of it for some time.

The stubbornness of high unemployment seems to strongly support the notion that Americans may be facing serious troubles ahead.

Signs of Oversupply

Very few small-time speculative investors have the knowledge or resources necessary to understand real market conditions. By the time they invest in condominiums, they may find themselves already in a saturated market, notwithstanding the fact that prices may remain relatively high for some time. The phenomenon of Baby Boomers moving into condominiums and steady immigration are contributing to the level of demand; however, the number of buyers purchasing condominiums as their principal residence is quite limited. When this number is exceeded by the number of units available and under construction, in the absence of speculative buying, the market becomes saturated.

In fact, whatever little demand remains after the market becomes saturated is maintained by some of the speculative investors themselves, most of whom are unaware that they are trading in oversupplied commodities primarily between themselves.

The most obvious sign of oversupply can be detected by

looking at the overall number of rental units in any given condominium complex. More than 30 percent of the units rented out or put up for sale is a fair warning to buyers of an oversupply of units. Conversely, if real estate agents are flooded with listings and many For Sale signs appear on front lawns, there is oversupply. It's a buyer's market.

As noted, oversupply may lead to serious adverse economic conditions. The real estate investment bubble eventually pops, often leading to a dramatic lowering of prices and an overall market recession. A slowdown in the construction industry leads to worker layoffs. Manufacturers of construction supplies follow suit by scaling down or ceasing operations, laying-off workers in the process. Electricians, plumbers, carpenters, and other trades find themselves without steady jobs, and many become unemployed. The entire economy is affected by job losses, which weakens consumer purchasing power.

Speculative investors may find that, in a slump market, they are unable to afford the carrying costs and maintenance fees on their units if they cannot rent them out at sufficient prices to cover the overall carrying costs. Even if their units are rented, they may find that, amidst the glut of other vacant units and rental apartments, their tenants may wish to move into cheaper rental condominium units or apartments, creating vacancies and contributing further to the likelihood that an investor will not be able to hold on to a unit.

Oversupply is almost inevitably a precursor to a downward trend in the real estate market. At the beginning of this trend, as previously noted, a decrease in condominium values may not be apparent for some months as many investors hang on to their units, often spending their last financial resources on carrying costs and maintenance fees. This is done in sheer desperation, hoping for a miraculous market turnaround. Such turnarounds seldom arrive. The survival of such hapless owners often depends on their financial strength outside real estate.

Buying Condos for Profit: Speculating

Ever-changing urban demographics and fluctuating real estate markets occasionally lend people the opportunity to invest in a condominium with the intention of selling it for profit. This practice is also known as speculating.

Properties are traded every day. During periods of high demand, some condominium owners may resell their condominium units in a relatively short time, sometimes even realizing a profit. Many such owners do not intend to live in their units for extended periods of time, and some do not live in them at all. They are taking a calculated risk that sometime in the future a new buyer will come along and purchase their unit at a higher price.

Many ordinary people become speculators during periods characterized by strong demand. There is a bit of a speculator in every one of us. We all wish to prosper; if buying a condominium unit offers a fair opportunity to make money, some of us will consider it. The aggressiveness of investors is determined by their level of courage and the amount of money (or credit) available. However, in any business the most important factor when it comes to taking calculated risks is knowledge of the business. Even the most experienced speculators lose money from time to time. You are strongly advised not to speculate in real estate unless you are knowledgeable, experienced, and, most important, in a position to absorb losses should your speculative venture turn sour.

Speculating in condominiums is a particularly challenging and often very hazardous activity compared with other forms of real estate. Some speculators do turn a profit, but their numbers are small in comparison with how many lose money. Ironically, the tenant residing in the speculator's unit is often the only one who enjoys the benefits of quality, carefree condominium living by paying a set, "worry-free" monthly rental.

The Perils of Personal Liability

In an adverse economy, liens on defaulted units and mortgage arrears may accumulate rather quickly, seriously diminishing the original unit owner's equity by the time the unit is sold. A defaulted unit's sale proceeds are reduced by the arrears of the overall debt and its interest and legal charges. This debt can reach a critical point in which no monies are left for the unit owner after the unit is sold. This occurs most often in cases where the unit owner bought their unit with little or no down payment. A shortfall or a loss resulting from the sale becomes a direct liability of the expelled unit owner.

In addition to losing the roof above them, and their

original down payment and closing costs, however small they may have been, owners are confronted with a monetary liability of a shortfall, because the unit was sold for less than what is needed to cover the debts incurred. Shortfall liability may haunt the ex-unit owner for years after losing a property. Until the debt is paid, they will deal with judgements, garnishments, and collection agencies, and suffer a tarnished record in their credit report files.

To avoid exposure and protect themselves from personal liability, some buyers purchase a unit in the name of a corporation. This may not entirely shield buyers from liability, because a personal guarantee is almost always required when applying for a residential mortgage. It may, however, provide protection from being personally liable for liens due to defaults on maintenance fees, assessments, or legal charges. If the condominium corporation insists on a personal guarantee – when foreclosed – the corporate shareholder will be stuck with the same amount of liability as if they had purchased the unit in their own name.

If the buyer's corporation can assume the existing seller's mortgage on the purchased unit without a personal guarantee, the shareholder of the corporation becomes entirely shielded from personal liability. In time, it will likely become evident that buying condominium units through a corporation without giving personal guarantees may be prudent even for those who consider themselves financially sound and secure.

By the same token, condominium corporations should be aware of losses that may occur as a result of defaults by corporate owners. Condominium bylaws should always insist on personal guaranties, regardless of how their units are owned.

CHAPTER 6

Recommended Reforms to the Condo System

Responsible governmental agencies should take the initiative to educate existing and future unit owners, as well as the public in general, about potential problems associated with condominiums. Changes should be made to condominium acts to make governments, the financial sector, developers, and the legal profession accountable to the consumer in these matters.

For example, developers should be required to obtain, and communicate, professional projections regarding the expected useful lifespan of condominium complexes, including the likelihood of all anticipated major repairs. Even though this information would not be construed as a warranty on the part of the developers, these projections, along with timetables showing future anticipated major repairs, replacements, and improvements, should be included in advertising and promotional materials for new condominiums, as well as in purchasing contracts.

It is important to stress again that low interest rates and high-ratio, mostly government-guaranteed mortgages have allowed low-income tenants with limited savings to become a new legion of condominium owners. While this may make them captive voters, they are not financially sound owners. Most of them can barely afford mortgage payments, maintenance fees, and taxes. If their financial circumstances take a turn for the worse, they likely will not be able to afford their monthly expenses, which will give rise to widespread default. Such buyers already comprise a large portion of condominium ownerships, leaving condo complexes exceedingly vulnerable to future losses. A sudden, even modest, increase in interest rates or unemployment may spell serious problems for those who invested little, or no, money in their units. Periodic market swings, sometimes known as corrections, can wipe out any equity they have in their units and cause serious hardships to remaining owners.

Following are my very specific recommendations for changes to the condominium system. They are based on the problems and challenges I have seen in dealing with consumers and the various parts of the condominium world itself.

Change the Quorum Required to Call a Special Meeting of All Unit Owners

From time to time, concerned and watchful unit owners may detect improprieties or neglect by board members that may cause the mismanagement of the complex. The problem is, these improprieties could occur at any time, but general meetings of all unit owners are held on a predetermined, regular basis, under the rules of the condo complex. What to do? Call an emergency general meeting of unit owners, of course. However, condo rules require that meetings outside the regular schedule may be called only if a certain percentage of unit owners can be assembled. That percentage, called a quorum, is usually very high, sometimes up to 85 percent.

This rule was originally meant to prevent whimsical and time-consuming meetings that could subvert the regular functioning of a board. Notwithstanding this, the percentage required for such a meeting needs to be lowered. Condominium corporations should amend their bylaws, and governments should amend their condominium acts, accordingly. I recommend that the definition of any quorum able to bring on major changes be lowered to 25 percent of unit owners.

These changes would enable meetings to be called quickly to deal with all sorts of problematic issues, including a budgetary crisis, indolent or non-performing board members, and any other matters that need to be corrected so the complex can safeguard its own interest and continue to operate as efficiently as possible.

The reasoning behind my recommendation is simple. Condominium corporations are unlike commercial corporations which trade in stocks and shares and are usually governed by a board chosen by the majority of their shareholders. The mandate of a condominium corporation is to preserve the value of *all* of the complex's units that people reside in and call their home. It is simply too easy, under present conditions, for a dysfunctional board to make wrong decisions that affect the whole complex.

Further, general meetings of all unit owners should be held on a mandatory quarterly basis, or even sooner if legitimate concerns or circumstances arise.

Notwithstanding the percentage of unit owners required to make *special* general meetings valid, a quorum of only 25 percent of all unit owners in regular meetings should be able to effect changes to bylaws, dismiss directors, elect new board members, cancel management contracts, and fire and hire professionals such as accountants and lawyers.

Mandate a Rainy Day Fee to Be Paid by Low-equity Unit Owners

I recommend that condo corporations mandate a mandatory rainy day fee (RDF) – a monthly surcharge to be paid by low-equity condominium buyers, added to existing monthly maintenance fees. The RDF should apply to any new unit buyer who purchases a unit with less than a 25 percent down payment. RDF fees would form a special fund, kept in a separate interest-bearing account by the condominium corporation to the credit of such unit owners. Corporations would be accountable to provide regular RDF account reports to the unit owners required to pay into it, including the account's outstanding balance and earned interest, the way they do with the reserve fund. The overall amount of the RDF should be shown on the Status Certificate.

Monies from an RDF would be used only when unit

owners fail to meet their financial obligations, such as payment on maintenance fees or special assessments. When the RDF accumulates to a sufficient level over time, it would soften the blow for the whole complex of any defaults of RDF-contributing unit owners. The corporation would not need to place liens on such units as long as sufficient RDF monies are available. This would eliminate legal costs and minimize problems associated with forced sale or foreclosure actions. The unspent portion of the RDF, along with its earned interest, would be returned or credited to the unit owner on the sale or other disposition of the unit. Owners who have paid into an RDF account could assign the amount they have paid to a buyer should they decide to sell their unit.

As for the amount that should be paid into the RDF account, I recommend, at minimum, 25 percent of the monthly maintenance fees payable each month. Requiring this extra payment would discourage buyers seeking to purchase a unit with a small or no down payment.

If the RDF cannot be mandated through amendments to existing condominium acts, it should be done through enactment of a new condominium corporation bylaw. Failure to make the obligatory monthly contribution toward the RDF should trigger the placement of a lien, with its usual enforcement mechanisms.

Require a Minimum 25 Percent Down Payment

As an alternative to the RDF, any prudent, well-governed condominium corporation should enact its own bylaws requiring its units to be purchased with a mandatory minimum down payment of 25 percent of the sale price. If this is in conflict with a condominium act, pressure should be put on legislators to amend the act, allowing corporations to enact their own bylaws in this regard. Corporations could also opt to mandate that condominium units cannot be mortgaged or otherwise encumbered for more than 75 percent of the appraised value of the unit at any given time.

The exception to that rule would be the necessity of refinancing the unit at the renewal date of the mortgage, if, due to lowering of the unit value, the owner is forced to take out a high-ratio loan. Such a unit owner would then become subject to the RDF fee.

This measure would minimize the possibility of massive losses caused by defaults on the part of low-equity owners during economic downturns.

A condominium complex is jointly owned by a multitude of individuals and indirectly by a multitude of other stakeholders such as mortgage holders and common loan lenders. The default of one unit owner automatically affects the rest of the non-defaulting unit owners. Unit owners with little or no equity pose a serious risk to the complex, especially if the complex is composed of a considerable number of such owners.

Traditionally, and particularly during volatile economic times, mortgage lenders did not consider lending on real estate unless a buyer can prove that they have at least a 25 percent down payment of their own monies. In the case of mortgages on condos, they sometimes require a minimum of 35 percent. This approach was intended to safeguard the equity position of the mortgage lender. Re-enactment of and strict adherence to this kind of policy will redound to the benefit of mortgage lenders, the condominium industry, and individual condo owners, especially non-defaulting unit owners by their becoming more likely to preserve the value of their units as a result of such a measure, in good times and bad.

It seems that, during the relative prosperity of the last decade or so, the financial sector and most condominium corporations let their guard down regarding risks posed by low-equity owners. Developers' zeal for a quick profit and the government's failure to protect taxpayers – the actual guarantors of high-ratio mortgages – may still lead to considerable losses to society. If such a trend continues, high-ratio mortgages will soon outnumber conventional mortgages, placing many condominium complexes in jeopardy at the first sign of economic trouble.

By mid-2010, mostly due to low interest rates and a relatively low unemployment rate, the real estate industry had experienced only a moderate rate of high-ratio mortgage defaults. As the banks' position is, relatively speaking, well secured due to taxpayer guarantees, this leaves condominium corporations, individual unit owners, and lastly, taxpayers, to bear the brunt once defaults start occurring on a large scale.

Bottom line, prospective condo buyers who can't put at least 25 percent down would be better off staying in their rented apartments or other living arrangements and saving their money until they can purchase real estate – and realize their investment's value – more safely.

Require Full Disclosure on Status Certificates

The "wellness" of any condominium complex is reflected in its Status Certificate (also known as the Estoppel Certificate), which is issued to the owner of or buyer of a unit from time to time by the condominium corporation. It is the only valid document of the actual wellness of the condominium complex.

I recommend that condominium acts be amended to make it mandatory that the Status Certificate list not only the financial affairs of the condo complex, but also:

- All current arrears regarding maintenance fees and special assessments

- Information on any existing or pending legal actions, insurance claims, and present and pending municipal and fire departments' orders or recommendations

- Any other deficiencies within the complex and the estimated cost to repair them

- Any need for future expenditures, whether real or anticipated, as well as the proposed method of paying or financing such expenditures

Each Status Certificate should be accompanied by a three-year audited financial statement of the condominium corporation along with an up-to-date statement within 90 days of the issuance, showing qualified projections in terms of real and anticipated expenditures for the following fiscal year and beyond if the expenditures require financing over a longer period.

I'm still not done. Condominium corporations should provide notices and directions in their Status Certificates that expressly authorize any bona fide buyer to make their own inquiries regarding outstanding or anticipatory work orders, legal actions, and/or any other matters concerning the financial status and well being of the complex. Complete disclosure and transparency is an absolute necessity for the potential condominium buyer.

Restrict Borrowing Against Receivables

I recommend greater limitations on condominium corporations' ability to obtain a common loan against receivables (special assessments, future proceeds from liens, and other revenues).

From time to time, a condominium complex may require larger sums of money to look after sudden major repairs or retrofitting. For instance, a condo corporation may need to spend substantial amounts on urgent unexpected structural or mechanical repairs. Because unit owners cannot contribute toward such a considerable cost at once, the corporation is forced to borrow money. This represents a common loan. It is repaid by higher monthly maintenance fees, which are pledged to the common loan lender as security for the loan. The liability against receivables assigned to the common loan lender is not only the liability of the condominium corporation, it is also, de facto, the individual obligation of all unit owners. Loans-on-receivables work to the benefit of the complex as long as their amount is reasonable in terms of the unit owners' ability to maintain and repay them on a timely basis.

To quote Mark D. Pearlstein, a noted Chicago-based legal expert on condominiums, "Under the terms of the (common) loan agreement, the Association lender receives monthly financial reports and thus is in position to recognize collection problems for the entire community. In that case, the lender will either take over assessment collection under an assignment or terminate the loan and force the Association to refinance. These steps will occur before a lender contemplates bankruptcy proceedings against the association."[13]

But what happens if the condominium corporation is unable to refinance its common loan, for example, during a bad economy when many condominium complexes experience financial difficulty because of a multitude of defaults by individual unit owners? Corporations may not be able to readily find another lender to refinance its common loan. This is where complexes with a considerable number of small or no-equity owners can get into serious trouble. Loans against a corporation's receivables may quickly become unaffordable and spell disastrous results to all unit owners. Failure to meet obligations on such loans may cause lenders to seek remedial collection procedures.

For example, in an extreme situation, a common loan creditor could sue the condominium corporation that

---

13 In correspondence with the author dated November 4, 2006.

defaulted and obtain judgement(s). The next step is receivership and bankruptcy proceedings against the entire complex, including collection proceedings against individual unit owners.

The corporation's loan on receivables is secured by special assessments and ranks in priority of the mortgages on individual units. The mortgage holder's position is immediately threatened by the default of a common loan. This is one of the reasons that mortgage holders will keep a keen eye on any defaults of common loans.

Borrowing beyond one's means is not uncommon. It happens every day to many of us. There is little or no reason to disregard the possibility that individual unit owners, individually, or collectively as a condominium corporation, may not succumb to the same weakness, especially if under pressure. The accumulation of common debt may become so high that, notwithstanding any outside economic factors, a complex may be faced with the possibility of its demise.

To protect themselves from such gloomy scenarios, condominium unit owners, as well as their mortgage holders, should insist on safeguards such as capping the corporations' ability to borrow against their receivables. The restrictions on borrowing should also be mandated and enacted by condominium acts and/or individual condominium bylaws.

Some responsible condominium corporations have become aware of this problem and have decided to restrict their borrowing to no more than 25 percent of their receivables. Any common loan should be approved by the majority of the unit owners. Such practices should become not only common practice, but also the law.

Compensate the Board of Directors

Most of today's condominiums are governed by a board of directors whose members are either poorly compensated for their work or not compensated at all. In many jurisdictions, the condominium act prohibits compensating directors, the rationale being that their work should be done on a voluntary basis because financial compensation would create unfair enrichment and inequity between unit owners and risk the homogeneity of the communal complex.

In fact, if you were to take a closer look at condominium and co-op ownership structures, a striking resemblance to a failed communist system would emerge, albeit at a micro-cosmic level. The land and the common elements of the complex are jointly owned by all the unit owners, who are expected to live by the same rules and equally contribute to the overall well being of the complex. In real life, however, this utopian system does not work. Some responsible corporations, in jurisdictions allowing compensation, have realized that and are now fairly reimbursing board members and other personnel involved with the governing of the complex.

Experience shows that fair compensation for board members is the only way to achieve a well-functioning, accountable, and responsible governing body.

As mentioned earlier in the book, most of the unit owners who elect themselves to positions on the board discover, over time, that the degree of personal sacrifice, time, and effort is much more than they bargained for. Eventually, long hours and the responsibilities of the job take their toll. Board members tire out and become disenchanted with their positions. Couple this with a lack of professionalism, and they are likely to leave important issues to be solved by an outside management company. Often, there is nobody left to closely monitor the management company's activities; however, it is pivotally important that board members monitor these activities. The management company may not be inclined, or able, to look after the interests of the complex to the same degree as the owners of the units.

It is not just that board members can become exhausted by their duties. It is also that they lack the knowledge to run a condominium complex professionally.

The only logical way to prevent board members from becoming apathetic and, therefore, ineffective, is to set aside a reasonable budget to reimburse them for performing duties in a most diligent manner. The rest of the owners would benefit from knowing that their board functions well. For most complexes, especially ones with more than 100 units, the benefits of receiving the best possible governance far outweigh the cost of compensating directors.

Condominium complexes should go a step further. They should hire an outside consulting firm to screen and check the references and qualifications of unit owners who wish to run for the board. Board members should have contractual tenures for their positions, such as six months to one year, with provisions for being fired if their work is not acceptable. Board members' performance should be monitored by committees composed of unit owners as well as outside independent consultants.

In that sense, a condominium complex should model itself after successful commercial firms that run apartment complexes. Good governance comes at a cost, but the lack thereof comes at a much higher cost.

CONCLUSION

Given the pitfalls of today's condominium ownership structure, addressed in detail in this book, you should be very cautious about buying a condominium to live in. You should be equally cautious in choosing the complex in which you intend to buy your unit.

Better yet, you might want to make a safer investment, i.e., buy a traditional home.

There is something to say for those who make the choice for their habitat, be it a traditional home or condominium. Such property owners are committed to their financial obligations with respect to the carrying costs of the property, regardless of economic changes, good or bad. These committed real estate owners strive to pay off their mortgage so they can eventually enjoy their property free and clear.

The traditional homeowner gets the better part of the deal in the long run, for, after paying off their mortgage, they are not left with the additional master deed burden associated with a condo unit owner.

As for buying property and assuming responsibility for

it, to maintain shelter for themselves and their family – this has been proven to govern and shape people's character. Preserving and enhancing the equity that they hold in their property breeds industriousness on a large scale; indeed, it forms the foundation of a prosperous society.

The History of Co-ops: A Cautionary Tale

Practically speaking, cooperatives and condominiums, by virtue of their ownership structures, are very similar forms of communal ownership. In both cases, while the individual units are used and enjoyed singularly, the rest of the residential complex is commonly owned.

The history of co-ops provides a cautionary tale. They were very popular in the roaring 1920s, but most plummeted into bankruptcy in the 1930s and, subsequently, most were converted into apartments.

Cooperative ownership involves one-tier ownership; condominium ownership involves two-tier ownership. But other than this legal, structural difference, the two are, physically speaking, similar if not identical. Co-ops have fallen out of favor, but many condominium owners have embraced the idea of an individually registrable unit, giving them (seemingly) the same comfort as owning a traditional property. This is the main reason that condominium owner-ship is so popular.

Cooperatives

To fully understand and appreciate the condominium ownership structure, you must examine the structure of its predecessor – the cooperative. Cooperatives are the father of communal ownership arrangements; examining them may reveal what lies ahead for their offspring, condominiums.

The first cooperatives in North America were built in New York City in the 1880s. They quickly became a popular choice for ownership accommodation, especially in the eastern and midwestern U.S. By the 1920s, cooperatives proliferated. Alas, most of them plummeted into bank-ruptcy or became insolvent during the Great Depression of the 1930s. Unit owners soon found themselves out on the street, their investment evaporated, as creditors swooped in to claim the buildings via various bankruptcy remedies.

Subsequently, these same buildings were converted into rental apartment buildings by new landlords, only to be reorganized again into cooperatives after the Second World War. However, because of the disastrous legacy of the 1930s, cooperatives never regained the momentum they previously enjoyed.

The cooperative is a simpler form of communal owner-ship than condominium ownership. The ownership arrangement of co-ops consists of a number of people owning a certain amount of shares or equity interest in the corporation or other entity, which owns the whole of the real estate property.

Most cooperatives are organized as corporations, much like any other corporate entity with limited liability. The corporation issues capital shares to individual unit buyers on a pro-rata basis proportionate to their investment in a particular unit. This allows the unit buyer to occupy that unit within the apartment building. Buyers do not directly buy the unit they occupy; rather, they acquire shares of the corporation that owns the property. Buyers of a cooperative thus become shareholders of the corporation and long-term proprietor leaseholders, though not the individual owners of their unit.

In return for buyers' investment or the purchase price, the cooperative association provides shareholder-purchasers with a proprietary lease for their particular unit, which, in some cases, may be time limited. In the absence of default, the proprietary lease for the unit is usually automatically renewed in perpetuity. It is important to remember that, in the cooperative form of ownership, the unitholder is not the actual owner of their particular unit but rather is the holder of a perpetual lease.

The responsibility of caring for the complex is left to the board of directors, also known as board members. The shareholders elect a board in a manner similar to any other corporate entity.

Inability to Mortgage

Some cooperatives are formed as nonprofit corporations. Some can also be formed as trusts or limited partnerships. Cooperative unitholders cannot obtain conventional mortgage loans on the individual units they occupy. Money can be lent only to the whole cooperative complex. Such loans become a joint mortgage liability on the entire complex, and the majority of the shareholders must agree to these arrangements. In real life, most cooperatives have already registered the underlying mortgage against the whole property, and a pro-rated share of the common mortgage is credited toward the unit purchase, thereby indirectly facilitating the acquisition of the cooperative unit.

Generally speaking, co-op buyers tend to be much more informed and aware than condo purchasers of possible financial perils arising out of the communal ownership structure. Usually, co-op unit buyers are well informed that they are to become shareholders of a cooperative corporation, governed not by the jurisdiction's condominium act but by its corporation act. Unit buyers can easily familiarize themselves with the laws pertaining to their involvement as shareholders in the cooperative corporation.

These common corporate laws have existed for many years and have been tested in court many times. From an investment point of view, cooperative unit buyers are investing money in a corporation of which they are part owner and occupier. Practically speaking, they become an asset owner of the corporation. Well-established legislation, as well as the internal bylaws of the co-op corporation, combine to determine, in a clear and understandable fashion, the individual owners' benefits and responsibilities.

Common Rules and Similar Lifestyles

Cooperatives are forms of communal ownership whereby all shareholders are expected to abide by the house rules and regulations and pay their pro-rated share of the common property's maintenance and care. This includes a pro-rated share in common element repair, maintenance and management costs, real estate taxes, and any underlying master mortgage or loans that may be registered against the complex. Such financial obligations are usually paid on a monthly basis.

The cooperative's board of directors scrutinizes potential buyers before they are allowed to buy shares. Responsible boards often go to considerable lengths to ensure that only the most compatible co-op buyers are approved so they become a good and valuable part of the commune.

The stringent rules for selecting suitable new co-op buyers are an absolute necessity. From a financial perspective, cooperatives are dependent on their fellow shareholders/unitholders. Other unitholders automatically assume liability if one or more unitholders fail to meet their financial obligations. When the economy is particularly volatile, the added burden and hardship created by the financial failure of others can seriously affect the co-op commune.

Severe Ownership Restrictions

The downside of cooperative ownership is that the stringent rules of selectivity and occupancy severely limit individual unitholders' rights compared with traditional forms of real estate ownership.

For example, cooperatives commonly forbid unitholders from renting their unit without the approval of the board of directors. The latter may employ stringent criteria in evaluating potential tenants, impeding unitholders' efforts in renting their unit and moving on. Unitholders may wish to rent their unit to a relative but be refused by the board. This type of restriction clearly demonstrates the limits of a proprietary lease ownership. This is the main reason that cooperatives are no longer popular. Other restrictions may include forbidding pets and not allowing friends or guests to stay overnight.

Numerically, co-ops are but a shadow of what they were in previous decades.

Easing the Rules Due to Desperation

Ideally, cooperatives consist of shareholders who are as much alike as possible financially and in terms of lifestyle. Purchasers of a cooperative unit voluntarily submit themselves to a regimen, knowing that they can expect the same sacrifice from their neighbors.

However, it is very difficult to create such an ideal communal group. Over time, people differ on many issues. Along with changes in the individual cooperators' financial status, the cooperative as a group and the security of the real estate it owns can be adversely affected.

If the cooperative becomes financially weak, either through mismanagement or a bad economy, its board may have no other choice but to become lax in imposing its rules with respect to new purchasers and renters. The cooperative complex, in financial difficulty due to the failure of a few unitholders, may find it difficult to attract new purchasers, which puts financial pressure on existing owners – sometimes to the point of liquidation and/or loss of equity. This scenario is an unfortunate reality for many cooperatives when the economy sours.

Powers are provided for the swift termination of the proprietor's lease and liquidation of a defaulted unit. These powers are for the benefit and survival of the complex. Potential purchasers of cooperatives are advised to think carefully before they buy into them. Careful examination of the cooperative's sense of financial well being is "must do" research before purchasing shares.

Only those who are content to live their lives based on the expectations of others should buy into a cooperative.

Bottom line? People looking into co-op ownership are turning their attention to a seemingly "better," "more secure" communal ownership arrangement – the condominium. But condominiums have their own share of serious communal ownership problems, as I have pointed out throughout this book. Understanding what happened to cooperatives can help us appreciate and evaluate present and future perils that lie ahead for condominiums. The knowledge can, and should, be used to prevent or minimize the future pitfalls that condo owners may experience.

REFERENCES

Aaron, Bob. (2006, July 22). Leaky condo lawsuit offers lessons for all. *Toronto Star* <http://www.thestar.com>.

Aulakh, Raveena, & Zlomislic, Diana. (2011, September 19). Condo fraud allegations shock family. *Toronto Star* <www.thestar.com/printarticle/1056432>.

Cyber Citizens for Justice Organization <http://www.ccfj.net/>.

Experian-Gallup (2007, April 1). Housing market recession and sub-prime mortgage market continue to affect confidence <http://personalcreditindex.com/Gallup_Archive_Content.aspx?id=25>.

Garcia, Beatrice, E. (2006, June 21). More insurers seek rate hikes <www.miamiherald.com>.

Gehrke-White, Donna. (2007, May 25). Condos: Kickback scheme could hit home, condo owners told <www.miamiherald.com>.

Grant, Tavia. (2007, June 15). Housing gets a lot less affordable. *Globe and Mail* <www.reportonbusiness.com>.

Haver Analytics <http://www.haver.com/>.

Kehoe Patrick, E. (1974). Cooperatives and condominiums. Legal

Almanac Series, no. 72 (p. 124). Dobbs Ferry, NY: Oceana Publications.

Levenfeld Pearlstein LLC <http://www.lplegal.com/our-people/attorney/mark-d-pearlstein>.

Mauldin, John <http://www.johnmauldin.com/> and <www.Frontlinethoughts.com>.

Matthews, Harry M. (1991). The condo/co-op owner's survival manual (p. 192). New York: Putnam.

Quealy, Kevin, & Tse, Archie (2011, May 11). Is it better to buy or rent?. *New York Times* <www.nytimes.com/interactive/business/buy-rent-calculator.html>.

Roseman, Ellen. (2006, July 9). Hidden costs a condo owner's nightmare. *Toronto Star* <http://www.thestar.com>.

Standard & Poor's. (2010, January 21). S&P/Case-Shiller Home Price Indices: 2009, A Year in Review <http://www.standardandpoors.com/indices/index-research/en/us/?type=All&category=Economic>.

U.S. Bureau of Economic Analysis <http://www.bea.gov/>.

U.S. Census Bureau <http://www.census.gov/>.

Webster, Bruce H., Jr., & Bishaw, Alemayehu. U.S. Department of Commerce, Economic and Statistics Administration. (2007). Income, earnings, and poverty data from the 2006 American community survey (ACS-08). Washington, DC: U.S. Government Printing Office.

CPSIA information can be obtained
at www.ICGtesting.com
Printed in the USA
LVHW021131091118
596395LV00022B/776